ANN ALLEN SHOCKLEY

An Annotated Primary

and

Secondary Bibliography

Compiled by
RITA B. DANDRIDGE

Bibliographies and Indexes in
Afro-American and African Studies, Number 18

GREENWOOD PRESS
NEW YORK • WESTPORT, CONNECTICUT • LONDON

Library of Congress Cataloging-in-Publication Data

Dandridge, Rita B.
  Ann Allen Shockley : an annotated primary and
secondary bibliography.

  (Bibliographies and indexes in Afro-American and
African studies, ISSN 0742-6925 ; no. 18)
  Includes index.
  1. Shockley, Ann Allen—Bibliography. I. Title.
II. Series.
Z8817.88.D36 1987   016.818′5409   86-33471
[PS3569.H568]
ISBN 0-313-25740-X (lib. bdg. : alk. paper)

Library of Congress Catalog Card Number: 86-33471
ISBN: 0-313-25740-X
ISSN: 0742-6925

First published in 1987

Greenwood Press, Inc.
88 Post Road West, Westport, Connecticut 06881

Printed in the United States of America

∞

The paper used in this book complies with the
Permanent Paper Standard issued by the National
Information Standards Organization (Z39.48-1984).

10 9 8 7 6 5 4 3 2 1

ANN ALLEN SHOCKLEY

CONTENTS

PREFACE

A critical inconvenience confronting scholars of Ann Allen Shockley has been the lack of an accurate or complete bibliography of published works by and about the author. Some of her works have been included in bibliographies and indexes, such as Carol Fairbanks and Eugene A. Engeldinger's Black American Fiction: A Bibliography (Scarecrow, 1978), M. Thomas Inge and others' Black American Writers (St. Martin's 1978), J.R. Roberts' Black Lesbians: An Annotated Bibliography (Naiad, 1981), and Theressa Gunnels Rush and others' Black American Writers Past and Present (Scarecrow, 1975). However, the need for an annotated bibliography of Shockley was so acutely felt by SDiane Bogus, a Miami University student writing her doctoral dissertation on the author, that is early 1985 she advertised for reviews of Shockley's fiction in several literary newsletters, including that of the prestigious South Atlantic Modern Language Association.

This bibliography was started two years ago for a course in Black Women's Studies which I initiated at Norfolk State University. The more of Shockley's writings I discovered, the more intrigued I became by the quantity and quality of her works and the relevance of these to black studies, women's literature, American history, and library resources. What initially was intended as a bibliographical essay on Shockley's writings has become an annotated bibliography of primary and secondary works. This comprehensive list of writings is intended to facilitate future research on Ann Allen Shockley and to allow for a full view of her writings and their critical reception.

This bibliography is arranged in four parts. Part I comprises citations and annotations of all the published and unpublished fiction of Ann Allen Shockley, up to and including 1985. Shockley's works in each category of fiction are organized chronologically to enable scholars to determine at a glance the subjects that interested Shockley at various times in her life. Short stories appearing in newspapers, periodicals, and the short story collection are separated for easy referencing. Part II presents citations and annotations of Shockley's published and unpublished nonfictional writings. This section is the larger of the first two parts because Shockley has written considerable more nonfiction than fiction. In Parts I and II, citations for unpublished works follow those for published works, and Shockley is referred to by her married name even though her early pieces, before her marriage in 1948, were written under her maiden name "Allen." All entries are numbered according to an alphanumerical system in which numbers prefixed with "A" are appended to works by Shockley.

Part III consists of the accessible reviews of Shockley's fiction and nonfiction, up to and including 1984. The reviews are arranged chronologically and grouped according to the arrangement of Shockley's works presented in Parts I and II. Part IV gathers and chronologically organizes the relevant biography and criticism of Shockley found in newspapers, periodicals, and books. It excludes indexes in which Shockley's name appears and omits published announcements, except when critical comments are included. The citations in Parts III and IV are numbered according to an alphanumerical system in which numbers prefixed with "B" are appended to works about Shockley. The annotations for all four parts were assembled from my collection of photocopies of works written by and about Ann Allen Shockley.

The annotations are abstract and descriptive, noting publication facts and commenting on drawings accompanying short stories in magazines and newspapers. I have chosen for these annotations the materials that interest me, but I have also quoted from primary and secondary works to enable authors to manifest their own sentiments. The varying lengths of the annotations for entries under any single heading reflect the relevancy and ranges of material dealt with and not my giving more attention to one work at the expense of another.

ACKNOWLEDGMENTS

My gratitude extends to many persons who assisted me in the completion of this bibliography. Ann Allen Shockley generously allowed me to examine her personal files and provided me with difficult-to-find information about her life and works. Susan Searing, Women Studies Librarian-At-Large for the University of Wisconsin System, and Joan Nestle, curator of Lesbian Herstory Archives, New York City, aided me in tracking down elusive citations to feminist-lesbian periodicals. Janet L. Sims, reference librarian at Moorland-Spingarn Research Center at Howard University, suggested a book-length publication for this study. Freddy L. Thomas provided technical assistance and Enoch P. Jordan and William R.H. Cloud proofread and made invaluable suggestions on the various drafts.

Others who have aided me considerably are reference librarians and archivists at Bridgeville (Delaware) Public Library, Enoch Pratt Free Library, Fisk University, Hampton University, Howard University, the Library of Congress, Maryland State Archives' Hall of Records, Norfolk State University, and Wilmington (Delaware) Public Library.

I extend thanks to Charles Rowell, editor of Callaloo, for granting me permission to use part of my review-essay "Shockley the Iconoclast," printed in the fall 1984 issue of Callaloo. I also acknowledge Black American Literature Forum, which will publish my selected bibliography of Ann Allen Shockley in its spring 1987 issue.

Finally, I am especially grateful to my students who patiently sat in my classes on the good and bad days as I worked on this bibliography.

INTRODUCTION

This is the first book-length bibliography on a black American woman writer, living or dead. Perhaps one reason for the neglect can best be summed up in Alice Walker's words, appearing in her foreword to Robert Hemenway's biography of Zora Neale Hurston: "America does not support or honor us as human beings, let alone as blacks, women, or artists." Similar to Zora Neale Hurston, Ann Allen Shockley, born June 21, 1927, is a black, a woman, and a writer; and like Hurston, during her lifetime, Shockley is relatively unknown on the national level, despite her recognition as a writer. She was the first black to write a newspaper column in Federalsburg, Maryland, and in Bridgeville, Delaware; among the first to develop essays regarding the care of black library collections; the first to co-author a directory of living black American authors; and the first black American woman writer to introduce in fiction a scorned and ostracized element in the black community-the black lesbian. Her worth can be measured by the total range of her writings as a free-lance newspaper columnist, fictionist, essayist, critic, and compiler. Her published works include two novels, a collection of short stories, more than three dozen uncollected stories, and a number of articles, book reviews, and essays; in addition, there are a librarian's handbook and a directory of black American authors, unpublished library manuals, two unpublished novels, and an oral history tape collection of Afro-American writers. Her latest work is an anthology of black women writers, scheduled for publication in 1987 by G.K. Hall.

For her substantial body of published writings, Shockley has received some recognition. She was given the National Short Story Award by the American Association of University Women in 1962, the Hatshepsut Award for literature in 1981, and the Martin Luther King Award in 1982 for her literary output. In 1975, she was granted an American Library Association Black Caucus Award for her work as first editor of the

Black Caucus Newsletter. She has been cited in numerous direc-
tories of American writers and has earned the plaudits of
such scholars and critics as Susan Koppelman, Calvin Hernton,
and Nellie McKay. Her contemporaries, writers such as
Pulitzer-prize winner Alice Walker and international scholar
Louie Crew, have also admired her works.

     Although Shockley has won major awards and positive
reviews from scholars and critics, her talent is still relatively unknown on the national level because of the obscurity
or loss of journals and newspapers she has contributed to.
Her feminist writings, for instance, have been restricted
to small, neonate alternate-press publications. These journals
are listed in Ulrich's International Periodicals Directory,
but few are held in university libraries or the Library of
Congress. The Louisville Defender, which Shockley contributed
to as a teenager, did not begin microfilming and preserving
its issues until 1951, six years after Shockley began writing
for it and eighteen years after its inception. Notations
penned on cut-out copies of Shockley's works published in
the Louisville Defender, which she kept in a scrapbook given
her as a teenager by her guardian, provided a source for
the incompletely documented entries from that paper which
appear in this bibliography.

     Shockley's talent is also relatively unknown on the
national level because of the thoughtless reviews some critics
have given her works. When Loving Her, her first novel on
an interracial woman-bonding relationship, appeared, former
Fisk University student and would-be poet Frank Lamont
Phillips, in Black World 24 (Sept. 1975), attacked Shockley
as a writer who "should know better" than to scribble such
"trash," and then consigned the novel to the dung heap by
writing, "This bullshit should not be encouraged" (B36).
This attack apparently was a retaliation for Shockley's poking
fun at an unknown, insignificant, and egotistical poet in
her short story, "Ah! the Young Black Poet"; Phillips seems
to have assumed that Shockley was belittling him after be-
friending him. Actually, the character in the short story
was a composite of all the young black poets that Shockley
had seen on Fisk's campus and elsewhere. Phillips' review
of Loving Her, for which he gained considerable attention,
seems to have been an unwarranted blow struck in anger, amends
for which he has attempted to make in recent years through
long-distance telephone calls to Shockley, during which he
has discussed his writings and works. In New York Native
2 (22 Nov.-5 Dec. 1982), another reviewer, Helen Eisenbach,
of a different race and sex than Phillips but just as reck-
less, having mistaken the racial identity of characters in
Shockley's second novel Say Jesus and Come to Me, completely
missed the satirical thrust of the novel and compared Shockley to a popular homophobic white woman (B52). About The
Black and White of It, Lynn Reynolds said, in Conditions:
Seven 3 (Spring 1981), she was unable to identify with the
book, and had no affinity with Ann Allen Shockley as a writer
(B15). Shockley did not take this narrow-minded and ad hominem
criticism silently. The mediocre reviews prompted her to
publish, in Sojourner: The Women's Forum 9 (Apr. 1984), a
professionally informative essay detailing criteria reviewers

should possess when critiquing new feminist or women-identified-women fiction (A264). Her response to these critics was typical of her dis-ease with others' myopic views and inhumane treatment.

Her unpopularity among critics, especially among black critics, has placed an unwarranted added distance between her and her more successful contemporaries, like Alice Walker, Toni Morrison, and Toni Cade Bambara, who have won the Pulitzer Prize, National Book Critics Award for Fiction, and American Book Award, respectively. Shockley has also written about the insidiousness, violence, and deceit black women encounter in macho, heterosexual, patriarchal, racist, white Christian America. But her women have not gone insane (Morrison's Pecola), attempted suicide (Bambara's Velma), or died (Walker's Mem). In her more recent fiction, Shockley's women have pursued an alternative life-style, one that has always existed in the black community, still does, and will continue to do so. Her exposure of the lesbian experience in black literature has placed her years ahead of her literary contemporaries, lifting the veil of this hidden aspect of black life, and adding a stinging richness to black literature whose subject matter in the last decade has become tainted with repetitiveness. A staunch feminist, Shockley has not humbled her writings with nursery rhymes or decorated them with epistle frames or stream of consciousness modes. She has written forwardly and boldly, obscuring nothing.

About her fiction and reviewers, she made the following observation:

> In writing, I am interested in conveying themes ....I am not into symbolism, allegory, folklore, imagery as such. Unfortunate, for these are the things reviewers love to tackle in books. Particularly the academician to prove how erudite he or she is. That's probably why [Jean] Toomer is so revered. He can be interpreted in so many ways, and he only wrote (published) one book. Academic word-play can be exercised. Ex.: James Baldwin was not writing about a tree, it was a phallic symbol; when actually he WAS writing about a tree. Reviewers forget that some of the authors whom they are injecting such profound meaning haven't finished college (Ann Allen Shockley, personal letter to Rita B. Dandridge, 31 Mar. 1985).

Shockley's statements have exposed very serious flaws in academic criticism: critics often read into a work what is not there, and censure what they do not want to be there; they deem acceptable some material written by male writers, but decry its use by women. Viewing Shockley's works from a narrow perspective, critics simply have overlooked the development of themes in her works and how these coincide with her various visions in different roles.

Her works generally have reflected her varied and often incompatible roles as critic and friend, satirist and humanitarian, feminist and devoted mother, teacher and

observer, Christian and non-churchgoer, black woman and
American citizen, straight woman and lesbian sympathizer.
She has written about integration and segregation, inter-
and intraracism, heterosexuality and homosexuality, fidelity
and infidelity, youth and age, conspicuous display and
poverty, and life and death. She has placed students and
a die-hard conservative college president in heated
confrontation, preachers' wives and battered whores in the
same church, and a woman preacher and her female lover in
the same bed. Often going against the grain of common thought,
some of her fictional pieces have evinced that the church
is not a haven for all sinners, the minister is not an earthly
deity, white colleges are not totally to blame for the black
"brain drain," and blacks are not always humane to others
of their race. An observer, lover, and liver of life, Shockley
has brought to her writing bold, honest and chewable food
for thought, impalpable to the average reader and ground-zero
thinker. She has written about what she has seen, felt, and
heard, seemingly not caring when others have not liked what
she has written, only being concerned when others have argued
that her subject matter did not exist or that it was not
appropriate subject matter for literature.

To understand Shockley as a writer, one must also consider the pressures that have confronted her as a part-time
author and full-time librarian. Of this strain, Shockley
confides:

> My writing hasn't developed in the way I think it
> should because I have to turn the creative processes
> on and off too frequently. That's why on Monday
> mornings, I am in a bad mood. I have to cut off
> everything but the mental act of writing, until
> Saturday. Then I have to recapture characters' minds,
> moods, relationships, speeches and settings all
> over again. I feel I should stay with them, be them
> until the work is finished, not have to give them
> up.
>
> That is probably one of the reasons why I prefer
> writing short stories to novels. I can be concise,
> make it [sic] compact and short. To write, I don't
> need an atmosphere like Yaddo or wherever. I have
> written short stories at the circulation desk [while]
> checking out books. When my children were babies,
> I had them on a schedule to fit into my writing
> habits. I am a disciplined writer. I have to be
> (Ann Allen Shockley, personal letter to Rita B.
> Dandridge, 31 Mar. 1985).

Shockley's enviable drive and stamina have been her
literary trademarks, traceable even to her early writing
career. She has been an avid reader and writer since the
eighth grade, where her Madison Junior High School teacher
Harriet La Forest discovered her writing talent. It was in
the eighth grade that she began thinking about the short
story form after examining Richard Wright's Uncle Tom's
Children. At eighteen, she published a succession of short

stories one summer in her hometown newspaper, the Louisville
Defender. She became fiction editor, feature story writer,
and columnist for Fisk University Herald, while pursuing
undergraduate studies at Fisk University (1944-1948). At
twenty one, in 1949, in Federalsburg, Maryland, she made
an unprecedented move in this conservative, small town when
she approached the white editor of Federalsburg Times about
including black-related topics in the white daily; she was
granted permission to write a weekly column. Repeating her
good results in Bridgeville, Delaware, in 1953, after her
marriage to William Shockley, a teacher in Seaford, Delaware,
she wrote a similar column in the white Bridgeville News
for approximately three years until the editor, under pressure
from "local bigots," asked Shockley to stop "editorializing"
(Ann Allen Shockley, personal letter to Rita B. Dandridge,
10 Feb. 1985). During the preparation of weekly newspaper
columns, Shockley submitted short stories to the Afro-American
[Baltimore] and the Pittsburgh Courier newspapers. From 1960
until 1965, while living in Bridgeville, she composed the
plots of such stories as "The Picture Prize," "A Far Off
Sound," and "Monday Will Be Better" while driving forty-one
miles every week day to Delaware State College in Princess
Anne, Maryland, where she worked in the college library.

From 1954 until 1961, with the urge to write somewhat
suppressed, she was tiringly busy. At various intervals,
during this seven year period, she raised two children,
William Leslie, Jr., and Tamara Ann, obtained a master's
degree in library science at Case Western Reserve University,
and performed her duties as assistant librarian at Delaware
State College. Although these years formed the longest hiatus
between her published writings, she did produce a monograph,
A History of Public Library Services to Negroes in the South,
1900-1955, in 1959.

This monograph was the first of many works on the library
which manifested Shockley's interest in neglected areas of
librarianship. Her essays on librarianship have reflected
her concerns and experiences as a curator of black collections, first at Delaware State College (1959-1960), then
at University of Maryland, Eastern Shore Branch (1960-1969),
and finally at Fisk University (1969-present). Initially
dwelling on in-house matters and then branching out to broader
concerns, these compositions ferreted out a multiplicity
of problems in maintaining special black collections, including book reviewing and ordering, research, relationships
between publishers and librarians, and the duties and responsibilities of librarians. The writings were constructive,
professional, and sincere exercises, and always included
guidelines for improvement. Their impact was all the more
forceful because Shockley not only documented problems, but
also offered solutions to them through her own research.
Regarding the problem of the lack of available information
on some black writers in black collections, for instance,
Shockley wrote the first biographical sketches of three relatively unknown but worthy black writers: Joseph S. Cotter,
Sr., Pauline Elizabeth Hopkins, and Red Jordan Arobateau.

With dogged determination, a voracious desire to read, and an insatiable urge to write, Shockley has published consistently and remarkably better and longer pieces since the 1960's, both fiction and nonfiction. Her initiative seems even more remarkable when one understands that during this period, she buried her father and half-brother on the same day, witnessed her children grow and leave home, watched her marriage disintegrate into divorce, and pulled up roots and moved from the Delaware-Maryland area to Tennessee. The years since the 1960s have included her two important published contributions to black collections, Handbook to Black Librarianship and Directory of Black American Authors, as well as her avant-garde Christopher Street, best seller list novels Loving Her and Say Jesus and Come to Me, and her controversial collection of short stories The Black and White of It. Of these, the former two works have brought her the larger reader audience and will probably be those for which she will be most remembered.

For permanent stature, Ann Allen Shockley needs to be evaluated in terms of her progressive aesthetic achievement in all of her writings. Over a period of four decades, she has narrowed her focus from general, sometimes trite, issues to specific and important human problems. She has abandoned the one-dimensional protagonist for the more realistic, multi-emotional one. And she balances opposing personalities more effectively. Her sentences have evolved from simple, unadorned clauses to multi-syntactically-related groups of words. Her wit and satire have taken on several levels of meaning, validating the complexity of human experience. Despite the increasing complexity of Shockley's works, the instructive element still appears, and it is more insistent, more informed, and more innovative. These worthy aspects merit attention, and regard for such universal qualities as these should place Ann Allen Shockley at America's literary door of acceptance, alongside other American writers.

ANN ALLEN SHOCKLEY

I.
FICTION WRITTEN BY
ANN ALLEN SHOCKLEY

STORIES IN NEWSPAPERS

A1. "The Little Church." <u>Louisville Defender</u> 7 July 1945: N. pag.

The first short, short story that Shockley published consists of fewer than three hundred words. It raised comments from some people who said that she was ridiculing the church, a misconception that stems apparently from the author's comparing the effects of the church to those of opium. Rather than satire, this piece is a single declaration that the church, like a medicinal herb, temporarily palliates the hurts inflicted by life and that the more people suffer, the more they depend on and become addicted to what eases the pain.

A2. "He Stayed for Dinner." <u>Louisville Defender</u> July 1945: N. pag.

The humor of this piece resides in the circumstances of Henry Jones, a poor black hungry preacher in a small Georgia town. His dilapidated church, located one block from the city dump, has few parishioners. On these he intrudes for his dinner. His method of obtaining food from Sister Jackson, who has just contributed to the remodeling of the church's roof, reveals a stance incongruous to his profession.

Flattery and lying are the schemes he resorts to. When he calls on Sister Jackson on Monday evening, knowing that her menu is chickken hash, he appeals to her womanly instincts by telling her she is the prettiest woman in his congregation. He lies that he is visiting her out of his concern for her welfare and allows her to believe that he is staying for dinner at her insistence. His annoyingly deceptive character is matched by that of his victim, Sister Jackson, who graciously entertains

her unwanted guest while vowing not to open the door
for him again. Whereas Henry Jones is typical of the
black preacher who becomes the butt of jokes in American
literature, here he is a more familiar character,
commonly labelled by southerners as one "who can eat
you out of house and home."

A3. "Her Eyes." Louisville Defender July 1945: N. pag.

Originating from an occurrence which the author observed
in a downtown Louisville restaurant, this short, short
story evokes images that can be described in idioms
related to sight. It centers in a poor, black woman,
probably a bag lady, who is a sight: "her hair was unkept
and nappy, and her dress was soiled and wrinkled." While
she does not possess acceptable social visibility, she
displays an act of kindness that is "out of sight."
Beyond all expectation, she gives to a blind beggar
one nickel of the two she possesses, while the elite
("the world's crusted cake") berates him and gives him
nothing. Her charity manifests her mental view of the
world which becomes the theme of this small composition:
man's inhumanity to man follows a frightening deficiency
of foresight.

A4. "I Stand Accused." Louisville Defender July 1945:
N. pag.

The first person narrator and protagonist is a loyal
Nazi on trial for murdering one hundred hostages to
avenge the death of one Nazi officer. His conscious
thoughts, interwoven with the judge's questions, reveal
his utter dislike for democracy and his worship of Adolf
Hitler as bearer of prosperity to war-torn Germany.
Knowledge of his impending death sentence does not lessen
his confidence in youth trained in Hitlerism, and his
labelling his judicial enemies as "fools" and "simple-
minded idiots" does not elicit sympathy. His calculating
first person thoughts are the reversal of those of the
author, who uses the Nazi for the purpose of reaffirming
her own views about the good of democracy.

A5. "Tuning In." Louisville Defender July 1945: N. pag.

The suggestive power of radio advertising is the focus
of this short composition. Correct timing, excessive
praise for a product, and a willing audience are the
keys to marketing the Masie's Liquid Sap commercial.
The victims are persons such as Kathy, the protagonist,
who comes home from work too tired to go out on a blind
date. Ironically, she becomes the "sap" for believing
in a commercial which claims to make beautiful a woman
who "looked like something that had a face like a mule
and a bark like a dog." Her gullibility acknowledges
the woman's victimization to tonics and cosmetics in
a commercial plastic society that glorifies youth and
beauty.

A6. "The Ways of Women." <u>Louisville Defender</u> July 1945: N. pag.

This is a witty prose sketch reminiscent of the 17th century Theophrastian character. Fat and overly dressed, middle-aged Lucille Gaggle assumes the characteristics of the supermarket fowl that interests her. Presenting herself to the butcher as an ordinary customer, rather than as the chicken inspector that she is, bears the weight of Shockley's earliest feminist attitude that a woman often employs duplicity to seek information and disarm her adversaries. Certainly the sexist notion that women are like senseless old hens is attacked.

A7. "With Malice toward None." <u>Louisville Defender</u> July 1945: N. pag.

What is significant about this 1940's piece is its positive statement about race relations. Not only is a World War II black soldier convinced of the fairness of the American judicial system, but persuades a white Army deserter to turn himself in. Affirming loyalty to America, the black soldier exclaims: "This is about the only place we can call our country. Even if things are tough in this place, there is at least a seed of justice that we are going to have to make grow. Take the courts for instance; we can appeal to them for help, and in many cases get it justly." Ironically, the black soldier places a higher premium on fighting for his country than his white counterpart. His position posits his sincere efforts to be accepted as a first-class citizen.

A8. "The Lord Is My Shepherd." <u>Louisville Defender</u> 1945: N. pag. Rpt. in <u>Fisk University Herald</u> 39 (Dec. 1945): 17-18.

"The Twenty-third Psalm," from which the title derives, becomes the prayer of Private Harris, who volunteers to bomb a German command post. His altruistic mission gives meaning to his experience which has had no previous purpose. He has always been watched by the law, is a bully to others, and has tried to dodge the army. His death allows others to live; and in their memories of him, he lives as an unselfish, kind, and patriotic soldier. In this sad short story, Shockley universalizes the war theme, sets it beyond the realm of racism, and envelops it with religious optimism.

A9. "The Eternal Triangle." <u>Afro-American</u> [Baltimore] 22 May 1948, Mag. sec.: 2.

"The Eternal Triangle" is the author's first short story in the <u>Afro-American.</u> The picture accompanying it is that of a man and a woman in a passionate embrace; this caress of love precedes a murder and belies the story's outcome. The tension in the story occurs when a married woman mistakenly pushes her lover from a cliff, a fate she intends for her husband, Jim, whom she hates. The intense darkness in which the murder takes place is a metaphor for the secret love the woman has harbored for her lover during her meaningless six years of marriage. That she is stuck with a husband whom she hates points to the inevitability of her misfortune, and her anonymity suggests the universality of her plight.

A10. "The Wise Buddha." Afro-American [Baltimore] 25 Dec. 1948, Mag. sec.: 7.

The plot of this story is built on a series of plausible coincidences necessary for Mrs. Buckingham, a well-to-do widow, to reunite with her daughter whom she banished from the house for marrying a poor postal worker. The unifying force is an antique gold Chinese Buddha purchased by Mrs. Buckingham but desired by her son-in-law for his wife's Christmas gift. In a fair exchange of favors between Mrs. Buckingham and her son-in-law, the magnanimity of the Christmas spirit is manifested. The newspaper editor's headnote to this Christmas story reads: Here's how a miniature statue of a gold Chinese Buddha brought real Christmas joy to one family...."

A11. "The Girl on the Bus." Afro-American [Baltimore] 2 July 1949, Mag. sec.: 6.

Compatibility as a prerequisite for marriage is the central theme. The epitome of incompatibility is embodied in the courtship of Marion and Harold. She is always tardy, while he is regularly punctual. Their courtship affirms the often-heard adage "opposites attract each other," but his calling off the marriage because she is late for the wedding asserts otherwise. Marian's subsequent and constant relationship with Tommy Davis, teacher at Kimberly College where he is called "the snail professor" because of his slowness, points to the necessity of finding a compatible mate.

A12. "Double Date." Afro-American [Baltimore] 10 Dec. 1949, Mag. sec.: 6.

The third person narrator effectively pokes fun at staid, pretentious members of academic life who often live cloistered dull lives. Protagonist Dr. Phillistine Brooks is, as her name suggests, an example of such persons. A reclusive English professor at a small college in Louisville, Kentucky, she maintains her pretentiousness until her unplanned night out on a double date with Dr. Brad Henry, a lively, unassuming physician. A well-wrought narrative with a fluid conversational style and comic tone, it has as its message that one can be introduced to life through excessive reading of books, but only by living life does one really get to know it.

A13. "The Set-Up." <u>Pittsburgh Courier</u> 14 Jan. 1950: 25.

According to the <u>Pittsburgh Courier's</u> short story
editor, all short stories submitted to this newspaper
should contain 1,200 to 1,500 words, deal with "all
phases of family life,... [contain] some interracial
flavor and [focus] preferably on the lighter side of
life." Shockley received the customary fifteen dollars
for the publication of this story.

"The Set-Up" is an engaging detective story about a
poor black man who answers a newspaper advertisement
for a gardener at the white Steward mansion and, upon
arriving, discovers the wealthy, white Valerie Steward
murdered. Told by Paul Dirks, first person narrator
and black suspect, the story from this perspective
enables the reader to grasp the nervousness, inse-
curities, and fright of an innocent man trapped in
a scheme of John Steward, the murdered woman's half
brother, whose motive for murder is to inherit the
entire half million dollar estate of his late father.
The circumstances and coincidences, so similar to those
in real-life cases where often the black man, because
of his color, is incarcerated, take a new twist here.
It is because Paul Dirks is black that he could not
possibly be Valerie's killer, a man whom John Steward,
when plotting his alibi, intended to be a white man
and Valerie's lover. That John Dirks is black provides
the comic relief required by the editors of the
<u>Pittsburgh Courier</u>, but such humor is fainthearted
since Dirks' innocence is established only by the care-
lessness of a cold-hearted killer.

A14. "The Curse of Kapa." <u>Afro-American</u> [Baltimore] 11 Aug.
1951, Mag. sec.: 8; 18 Aug. 1951, Mag. sec.: 3+.

"The Curse of Kapa," Shockley's only serialized newspaper short story which appeared in two issues of the
<u>Afro-American</u>, begins and ends with a frame. The frame
introduces Maritha Mullock, who relates her adventures
on the strange island of Capah to her unnamed narrator
friend, at a chance meeting in the Koran, a Louisianna
restaurant. The frame emphasizes Maritha's contact
with the real world after being held a prisoner on
the mysterious island of Capah, named for her first
husband Julius Mullock, believed to have been blessed
with eternal life by Kapa, the island's evil spirit.
Between these framing scenes, Shockley creates a life
of terror for Maritha, plagued with a dismal life in
an alien land. The mysterious death of her first husband, the catatonic affliction of the second, the re-
appearance of the first husband in the image of the
second husband and of her son are woven into a tale
of mystery and suspense. Entrance into this sur-
realistic world is provided by the strange, dreamlike
setting of the restaurant, located "just off the main
street underneath an old rooming house" and lit by
candles "casting quivering shadows in the corners."

Shockley avoids making Maritha's story totally unbe-
lievable through the use of several ploys, foremost
of which is the question-answer technique. The narrator's interrogation of Maritha reveals the latter's
son has become a prominent minister and that the island
of Capah was destroyed by Japanese invasion during
the war. The narrator's skillful interrogation and
attentive listening are primary ingredients in feature-
story writing, an avocation Shockley practiced well.

A15.   "The Champ Bows Out." Afro-American [Baltimore] 8 Mar.
        1952, Mag. sec.: 8.

This story is a sensitive and fast-moving account of
an aging boxing champion who, in order to hasten his
retirement, allows the Kid, his younger opponent, to
win the championship. The setting is a boxing ring
during the championship fight, the details of which
are effectively told by an omniscient narrator. Important to an understanding of the champ's bowing out
is his own realization of the inhumanity of the sport
and his lack of concern for the money it brings and
the excited crowds it draws. The reader is left with
the idea that the new champion keenly senses the predicament of his older opponent and that he, too, within
a short time, will experience the same dilemma.

A16.   "Rover Was His Rival." Afro-American [Baltimore] 22
        Mar. 1952, Mag. sec.: 12.

An amusing piece casts a house-broken pet as a husband's
rival. It shows that by excessively loving a dog while
simultaneously ignoring a spouse, one can alienate
a human relation and strain a marriage. Allowing a
silence to wedge between a husband and wife, Shockley
justifies the husband's attitude that dogs are not
human and questions the commonly-held notion that "The
dog is man's best friend."

STORIES IN PERIODICALS

A17. "The Picture." Fisk University Herald 39 (Nov. 1945):
      15-16.

      Passing is the theme of this short story in which John,
      renowned concert pianist, keeps hidden from his white
      wife and from the world his black ancestry. His wife's
      discovery of a photograph depicting him as a boy in
      the arms of his black grandmother provides the tension
      in the story. The anxiety is resolved in the solution
      the wife proposes to her husband's problem: "the only
      way that racial prejudice can be broken is by each
      member of your race being individuals." The wife's
      loyalty to her husband, despite his racial difference,
      gives this "passing" story a hopeful ending, unlike
      traditional stories containing a tragic mulatto char-
      acter.

A18. "The Waiter." Fisk University Herald 39 (Dec. 1945):
      16-17.

      This story has no conventional plot or narrative action.
      The plot, if one can call it that, presents a young
      waiter at Enrico's International Hotel observing the
      pettiness and gaudiness of the rich as he serves them.
      He serves his customers graciously; however, the con-
      flict emerges when the waiter's inner feelings manifest
      his hatred for his patrons. Despite their smug attitudes
      about each other, the "served" and the "servers" are
      interdependent. This story gives a glaring view of
      the superficial estrangement of human beings despite
      their mutual dependence.

A19. "Song of Hope." Fisk University Herald 40 (Oct. 1945):
      26-29.

      "Song of Hope" is a moving love story without a happy
      ending. It details the love of a hopeless blind white
      poet for a beautiful black girl who sings "The Song
      of Hope." The singer's refusal to accept the poet's
      marriage proposal explains the latter's triple blind-
      ness. The white poet is physically blind, unperceiving
      that his lover is black; he is racially ignorant that
      a black can sing about positive subjects; and he is
      chauvinistically oblivious to the fact that a woman
      would refuse his offer of marriage. After all, he tells
      her, "I'm free, white and over twenty-one." Obviously,
      the theme is that prejudicial blindness is more of
      an affliction than either physical blindness or ethnic
      and gender inferiority. This interracial love story
      is the author's earliest statement on the inability
      of love to survive racist, sexist tension.

A20. "Living in Fear Is a Slow Death." Fisk University
      Herald 40 (Jan. 1947): 8-10, 24.

      Exploring the emotion of fear, this story functions

as a companion piece to "Song of Hope." It depicts an unnamed protagonist whose life is dominated by fear. In her obsessive-compulsive neurosis, the victim constantly looks behind her fearing that someone, especially a man, wants to attack her. Her toying with "a loose string in the lining of her pocket," as she walks the streets, suggests that her emotional conflict stems not only from an imagined attack, but also from her wanting to caress and be caressed. That she has no male friend contributes to her unhappiness and renders more plausible her unreal world of terror. Her suicidal leap from the ferris wheel into space actualizes her panic in fear-confronting situations and points to her ultimate mental incapacitation.

A21. "Abraham and the Spirit." Negro Digest 8 (July 1950): 85-91.

A sketch of a minister standing on bare, uneven floor boards accompanies this story in Negro Digest and graphically illustrates its contents. A satire on hypocrisy of black church folk, the story is an early account of what becomes Shockley's life-long view of deception in the church. The setting is a Sunday church service during which twelve-year-old Abraham, seated on the mourner's bench, tries hard "to feel the spirit," while his grandmother, angry that he has not quickly accepted Christ as his savior, hastens Abraham out of his seat toward the alter by sticking a hat pin in his buttocks. Her intolerant act climaxes a series of intolerant doings in the story and symbolically dramatizes the insufferable nature of some church-going Christians.

Realism underscores the satire, thereby rendering believable the presented material. Shockley faithfully presents the call-and-response recitation between congregation and minister and then targets the worshipers fidgeting to get out of the hot, stuffy church after the sermon. She paints the preacher as an impressive, erudite figure rendering a thundering sermon on lost sheep, but then ridicules his imperceptiveness when he mistakenly welcomes Abraham as a found sheep. Abraham, as the central character questioning the reality of the spirit and the meaning of Christianity, becomes a literary complement to protagonists Tisha Dees, in Arthenia Bates Millican's novel The Deity Nodded (1973), and John Grimes, in James Baldwin's novel Go Tell It on the Mountain (1953). He, like them, challenges guarded beliefs about black folk's faith and even questions the presence of genuine religious ecstasy.

A22. "Bad Girl at Large." Tan Confessions 1 (Mar. 1951): 17, 60-62.

Short stories written for Tan Confessions were required to be true stories and were penned by professional writers whose names did not appear with the stories they wrote. This story is based on a realistic situation familiar to Shockley, who centers its interest in the unstable consciousness of naive Robert Parker. Parker, the narrator, reflects on his recent extramarital affair while waiting for news of his wife's condition at a city hospital, after her attempted suicide. From his perspective, the reader is made aware of his seduction by Lona, his wife's younger sister; his adultery and subsequent request for a divorce; his wife's depression and suicidal attempt; and Lona's jilting him. The story has all the ingredients of a modern short story, and the circumstances convey Robert as a pathetic character.

Robert's early approach to the triangular affair is a demonstration of his regard for and belief in the commandment, "Thou shall not commit adultery," that he has worked out within himself in his naive manner. He assumed that Lona's games would only progress so far and, therefore, he would not run the risk of breaking a moral law; after all, he had a "normal, happy married life." He misjudged Lona and underestimated his own weakness. Summarily, the story dramatizes the lack of trust between the sexes. The more specific focus, however, is the gullibility of man who demonstrates an incredibly careless chauvinism, a lack of sophistication in handling a sultry teaser, and the failure to keep the marriage vows sacred.

A23.   "The Picture Prize." Negro Digest 11 (Oct. 1962): 53-60.

"The Picture Prize" probes the emotional scars that a quasi-integrated southern society has on James Henry, a young black elementary school boy who wins first prize in a children's art festival but is not allowed in the all-white museum to unveil his work of art. Since blacks are only allowed to visit the museum in July, James' prize, a silver cup with his name on it, is presented to him on the museum's steps, a ceremony that mocks his talents rather than honors them. The unveiling of his drawing reveals his original work of a naked black boy crying red tears while standing in the midst of greyness on a dark road. This portrait captures James' frightening encounter one night with drunken white men who harassed him while he was enroute to the canning factory to take his father his dinner; but it also becomes a fitting metaphor for James' general dismay over the racial situation.

The picture accompanying this story in Negro Digest is that of a black boy wearing a tight-fitting bow tie. It epitomizes James Henry's choking experiences as a black boy in white America. It comes as no surprise that his emotional lynching manifests itself in withdrawal: he never goes to see his picture hanging in the art gallery, "not even when colored were allowed."

A24.   "A Far Off Sound." Umbra 1 (Dec. 1963): 11-17.

The importance of this story is its portrayal of a New England white woman as a scapegoat for the insensitivity whites demonstrate toward blacks. Clarissa, the protagonist, represents the typical condescending white person who indiscriminately labels blacks as good singers, dancers, and athletes. She stereotypically tags Nikodemus, a black Alabama star basketball player, whom she sexually admires. For the sacrificial ceremony, he removes her from a soft stool in a Manhattan bar, where she drinks martinis, to the hard floor in a black apartment, where she gags on a chitterlings dinner at a rent party. This spatial metaphor, with its contrasting worlds of comfort and discomfort, dramatizes well the social-racial fissure in America.

A series of descriptive details affirms the denigration of the white woman and the elevation of the black man, important ingredients in this sacrifice. In an ironic reversal, Clarissa becomes the ignorant, gaping spectator during Nikodemus' ritualistic storytelling of how his father was killed in Alabama for allegedly raping a blond, blue-eyed woman, whom Clarissa reminds him of. Clarissa's nakedness, both sexual and intellectual, is left exposed; her condescending position, harassed and weakened. Her flight from the blues-filled room into the dark without denying her guilt is her admission that any attempt to establish her innocence is beyond her reach. The magnitude of whites' injustice to blacks will weigh on her as does the immensity of "the far off sound" of the blues played by Count Basie and Joe Williams.

A25.   "Monday Will Be Better." Negro Digest 13 (May 1964): 54-65. Rpt. in Impressions in Asphalt: Images of Urban America in Literature. Ed. Ruthe T. Sheffey and Eugenia Collier. New York: Scribners, 1969. 227-43.

"Monday Will Be Better" contains one of Shockley's important statements on de facto segregation in the public school system in the South. The story is concerned with whites' unreadiness to deal with school integration in the 1960's and their use of senseless tactics to deny blacks equal opportunity to education. The tension in the story centers in the white middle-aged teacher, Mrs. Banks, and James P. Johnson, her token black pupil whom she slights despite his intellectual capabilities. Her presumed racial superiority reveals itself in her surname "Banks." Her prejudiced attitude revolves around the belief passed down by her father -- "blackness is a gauntlet, the albatross around the white man's neck."

Mrs. Banks' adherence to a racist tradition is metaphorically realized in her daily routine: during the spring and fall she wears a white sweater and in the winter, a white coat. Her reluctance to change her clothing habit is as visible as her unwillingness to rid herself of her "old black Ford of questionable age." Representing an old order giving way to the new, she experiences headaches symptomatic of the tension necessary in a stressful situation involving change.

She reluctantly surmises that Monday will be better
for James, who eventually gains acceptance from his
white classmates one weekend after he wins the football
homecoming game.

A26. "The Funeral." Phylon 28 (Spring 1967): 95-101. Rpt.
in Out of Our Lives. Ed. Quandra Prettyman Stadler.
Washington: Howard UP, 1975. 274-85.

The dominant imagery in this story is death -- isolation, sickness, deterioration and dissipation. This
imagery weaves through a plot in which Miss Eliza,
an arthritic and diabetic octagenarian, dies of a heart
attack, leaving behind her granddaughter Melissa, the
only known relation, an alcoholic loner. The sadness
of this old woman's death is magnified by the long
destitute life she lived in order to have a grand funeral.

Satirizing the funeral's pomp, Shockley enables the
reader to realize this sadness. The juxtaposition of
the ostentatious funereal preparations with the poverty
of Miss Eliza's life underscores all the more her
trivial existence. The Cadillac hearse and lace-embroi-
dered shawl belie the fact that Miss Eliza was a poor,
black southern woman who attended other people's fu-
nerals so that hers would be attended. The simile "she
had been a fixture in the town like the Confederate
soldier in front of the court house" alludes to the
racial, sexist, and legal barriers which confronted
her as a second-class female, southern black citizen.
To Miss Eliza's way of thinking, her precarious existence validated the controls she exercised in meticulously planning her own funeral. Ironically, she lived
to die; she found rest at death. Melissa's sitting
in her grandmother's rocker with gin bottle in hand,
at the story's end, suggests that her life will follow
the insignificance of Miss Eliza's until the "next
funeral which will come in the manner of a charging
white horse to interrupt the dull monotony...."

A27. "Ain't No Use in Crying." Negro Digest 17 (Dec. 1967):
69-78.

Set in Mississippi in the 1960's, this story describes
the curious relationship between race and sex and
intensely explores the psychological conditions of
the principal characters, white and black. Fifteen-
year-old Carrie Mae, a good-looking, poor black girl,
is nearly raped by her white neighbor, Mista Bust Will,
who takes her to his home under the pretense of wanting
her to attend to his children. Shockley stops short
of the rape because she is more interested in the mental
make-up of the characters than the sexual act itself.

At the center of Bust Will's thoughts is the notion
that black girls are sexually easy to be with. He pre-
sumptuously assumes that Carrie Mae at fifteen has

been with many black fellows in the bushes and that she will engage in sex with him also. That she is not allowed to date because her mother is a strict disciplinarian never occurs to him. Bust Will's erroneous assumptions about her are magnified when balanced by the naivete of Carrie Mae, who questions what he wants with her. And his assumptions attest to the regional, racist, and sexist attitudes of the white men who have eyed Carrie Mae and hurled lewd remarks at her. His attitude is upheld by the law represented by a hypocritical sheriff who fails to investigate the case but displays in his office a poster revealing the American flag and the words "LIBERTY AND JUSTICE FOR ALL." Shockley adequately captures the southern drawl and attitude in the sheriff's remarks to the mother: "Ain't no nigger coming in muh office with any old ac-cu-sa-shon like that. Ain't a whi-ite man in this town who'd even bother with any old nigger gal!... Now git outta mah office before ah put both your black asses in mah jail." His words reveal the deeply prejudiced belief that a white man, no matter how trashy he is, is too good for a black woman; and that the black woman has no right to guard against an attack on her person. The mother's words to her daughter are equally dramatic: "Ain't no use in crying now." Ironically soothing and harsh, these words are the only protection a black mother can offer her sexually developing daughter, violated by racial bigotry. A blend of local color and historical fact makes this an unforgettable narrative about unprotected southern black womanhood.

A28.   "End of an Affair." <u>Liberator</u> 9 (June 1969): 14-16.

The interracial love affair between Keith, a married white man, and Nadine, a single black woman, is the subject of this narrative. The story has a modern setting, but the plight of Nadine seems no different from that of her countless black foremothers who have served as "sperm receptacles" for white men. The money Keith offers Nadine at the end of their two-year affair, when his wife discovers the liaison, checks Nadine's role as potential wife and demotes her to prostitute. The macho, uneven way the relationship has developed is seen in the possessions Keith maintains--wife, sons, business, and good name, all of which contrast sharply with Nadine's losses, which include her job, friends, and self-respect. Nadine's pregnancy is not an asset; it entraps her in further despair, escape from which she kills herself and Keith.

This suicide-homicide serves three purposes: to end the immediate relationship, to avenge her foremothers snared in illicit interracial relationships, and to sign off the black woman's being made a sexual toy in the future. The "grotesque death pattern of love-making," which the two dead bodies form, signals to society that these two lived as they died -- in sexual embraces. This death position brings to light the secrecy of the affair and Nadine's ultimate triumph over Keith.

A29.   "To Be a Man." Negro Digest 18 (July 1969): 54-65.

"To Be a Man" delves into the psychology of a black man trying to sustain his manhood in racist America. Claude, the main character without a last name, is symbolic of the invisibility, ineffectualness, and powerlessness that have been the historical legacy of the black man in America. Disenchanted with his bourgeoise background, he drops out of college, grows an unruly Afro and beard, works for the Movement earning ten dollars a week, and writes anti-white manuscripts which publishers return. His predicament is summed up by psychiatrists William Grier and Price Cobbs in Black Rage in this manner: "For the black man in this country, it is not so much a matter of acquiring manhood as it is a struggle to feel it his own. Whereas the white man regards his manhood as an ordained right, the black man is engaged in a never-ending battle for its possession."

Ironically, Claude has to battle for his manhood on his own turf. In a Harlem bar, he strikes out at Bull, a white cop who maliciously beats him during a search for another black man who has mugged a white man nearby. That the white man can stalk black territory while the black man remains vulnerable to abuse in his own territory is best borne out in an explanation of the cop's nickname, "Bull." The name suggests not only that the policeman is a bully, but also that as a white man he possesses a penis, a symbol of strength. "This biological affirmation of masculinity and identity as master," state Grier and Cobb, "is enough to ensure that, whatever his [the white man's] limitations, this society will not systematically erect obstructions to his achievement."

The climax to the story parallels Claude's orgasm as he rapes his wife in a fit of anger after being beaten by cop Bull. He uses sex as armament; it is his only reasonable and conscious means of defense. The darkness in which the rape occurs metaphorically suggests his secret battle with the white man, and his anger transferred to his wife is Shockley's strong articulation of the black woman's methodical and systematic victimization in the black-white racial war. Claude's ultimate defeat comes when his abused wife tells him, "It takes more than that to be a man." Retreating in sleep to the unsavory recesses of his mind, he parallels two other well-known battle scarred protagonists in black literature who have retreated to sewers, namely the unnamed narrator in Ralph Ellison's Invisible Man and Fred Daniels in Richard Wright's short story "The Man Who Lived Underground."

A30. "The President." Freedomways 10 (Fourth Quarter 1970):
      343-349.

      The setting for this story is the office of the presi-
      dent at a small black college. The occasion is a con-
      frontation between black student activists and the
      college president, an occasion reminiscent of student
      uprisings on black college campuses in the 1960's.
      The debate between the students (representing black
      nationalism) and the president (representing integra-
      tion) is more than a race issue. It becomes a human
      dispute fueled by the clashing ideas of youth and age,
      change and stability, independence and dependence,
      impatience and patience. The story climaxes when the
      president sadly realizes he is no longer needed by
      the younger generation and compares himself to an old
      tree whose leaves (the students) desert him in an au-
      tumnal blast. The writer's sympathy seems to reside
      with the president, not necessarily for what he repre-
      sents, but for the respect he does not receive for
      services rendered. The manner in which the students
      disrespect their president provides the story's inter-
      est.

A31. "Is She Relevant?" Black World 20 (Jan. 1971): 58-65.

      Is she relevant? is a question probing the significance
      of a white woman in a romantic relationship with a
      civil rights activist. It reflects the concerns of
      black men and women who have watched their black social
      and political leaders "talk black but sleep white"
      during the Civil Rights Movement. The question is
      a practical one because it embodies the fears and mis-
      trust of those who have been indoctrinated to believe
      in one line of political thought, but later discover
      the hypocrisy of those whom they pledged to follow.

      The theme of hypocrisy is advanced by the actions of
      Eli, who fronts as a soul brother, but lives high with
      "his own white broad." In the presence of his black
      audience, he dons a "mountain high...Afro hairdo,"
      displays a colorful dashiki, gives the clenched-fist
      symbol for power, and booms "Black Power" into the
      microphone. Unknown to most of his constituents, he
      drives a red jaguar, lives in an expensive hotel, and
      keeps a white mistress. Procuring devotees for the
      Movement puts money into his pockets and finances
      his interests in the white world. Success at his game
      depends on his keeping his two lives separate.

      Eli's double life is his attempt to exist as a whole
      person in segregated America. Being less than a whole
      man is metaphorically realized in the absence of his
      last name. Struggling internally with his fragmented
      existence, he ponders his definition for accomplishment,
      compared to that of the white man; questions the mar-
      riageability of his white woman; and admits his sexual
      appetite for a black woman. The white woman, however,

is very relevant to him because she feeds his ego and
gives him a place in the white world he would not otherwise have.

A32.   "Crying for Her Man." Liberator 11 (Jan.-Feb. 1971):
        14-17.

The disappointment of romantic love becomes the central
theme in the episode involving Thomas "Flash" Jackson
and his wife, Bonnie. Contributing to this disappointment is "Flash's" incredibly mercurial nature, which
oscillates from handsome prince charming to drunk,
wife beater, and rapist. The depravity of his trans-
formation manifests itself in his raping his wife
pinned against the kitchen wall after beating her for
withholding money.

Bonnie's prostration against the wall symbolizes her
sexual submission and her abasement as a woman who
cannot maintain her ideal of femininity. The wall becomes the whipping board of sex, her prison from which
she cannot escape because "Flash's" life is kept alive
by his sexual prowess. The lyrics, "the blues ain't
nothing but a woman crying for her man," become an
appropriate metaphor for Bonnie's predicament; they
record her despair at the realization that she is
married to one of many black men who are but "dark
specters...kept alive by the phallic symbol." The story
dramatizes well the interconnecting relationship between
sex and violence.

A33.   "The Faculty Party." Black World 21 (Nov. 1971): 54-
        63.

"The Faculty Party," a timely story, is one skill-
fully written with engaging dialogue. The interchange
and discussion of ideas that take place between the
characters form the bulk of the action which occurs
at a party given by the president of a prestigious
midwestern college for new faculty members. The conversations that ensue between two black faculty members,
Paul Wood and Dave Fry, give another view of a frequent
and painful phenomenon of the 1960's -- the defecting
of black faculty members from black colleges to teach
at white universities.

In the conversations that buttress the action, Shockley
does not dwell on venal white academicians draining
the black "brains" from black colleges; instead, she
reveals the black professors' reasons for defecting.
Both characters defect in the interest of self-better-
ment, but ironically neither betters himself by defecting. Both professors debase themselves as profes-
sionals. Dave Fry prostitutes his academic talents
by writing garbage in scholarly journals; as his surname
"Fry" suggests, he knowingly electrocutes himself aca-
demically. Similarly, Paul Wood prostitutes his moral
integrity by staying married to his nymphomaniacal

wife. His surname "Wood" appropriately suggests the
forest of pity he loses himself in as he cries hysteri-
cally upon discovering his wife with a blond man. These
two characters enable Shockley as a social critic to
explain that white colleges should not bear all the
blame for luring blacks -- as was the accusation in
the 1960's --because some blacks sought out white
colleges as an escape from the pressures in the black
community. The importance of this piece is the seldom-
expressed view that many blacks did themselves a dis-
service when they defected to white colleges.

A34.   "Her Own Thing." Black America 2 (Aug. 1972): 58+.

Interracial role reversal dominates this non-dramatic
plot with a one-day setting, in which two middle-class
black housewives, supported by their successful hus-
bands, assume the roles of suburban white women. Role
reversal becomes a therapeutic experience for Afro-
coiffeured Edmonia. She gains self-respect, rids herself
of jealousy for the white woman and her possessions,
and decides to do her own thing by reentering the job
market as a nurse. Her disenchantment with her life
is reflected in the vulgar pun she uses to refer to
her husband's relationships with whites: "he's getting
more like them each day. Association brings about ass-
similation."

Role reversal is an affliction to Stell, Edmonia's
soap opera junkie-companion. Equating her liberation
to the amount of support her husband gives her and
the children, she resembles the welfare mothers she
despises. Like them, she dissipates her youth by drinking and smoking excessively, gorging herself with junk
food, and limiting her education to television shows.
She is weaker than Edmonia owing to her inability to
recognize her personal conflict. The story vividly
illustrates the pitfalls in a situation often regarded
as utopian to an outsider.

A35.   "A Special Evening." Sisters 4 (Aug. 1973): 18-28.
Rpt. in The Black and White of It. Tallahassee:
Naiad P, 1980. 97-103.

The dominant metaphor in this short story is rain,
sometimes heavy, sometimes blinding. Strategically
placed references to downpours within the story are
crucial to understanding Toni Reis, a lesbian surgeon,
whose internal frustration and tension mount when heavy
rain nearly ruins a special evening on which she plans
to dine out with Letia, her patient-friend. Just as
the internal uproar produced by past experiences of
hurt conflicts with statements Toni would like to make
to Letia, so does the noise from the downpour compete
with the hi-fi music. The intensity of Toni's emotions
is best exemplified in the awkward expression "the
rain's hoofbeats against the window galloped in tune
with her heart." Only when the rain subsides does Toni

admit that she likes being with Letia and her fear
of others discovering her as a lesbian lessened. The
rain metaphor effectively dramatizes the discomfort
of the closeted lesbian in unfamiliar territory.

A36.   "The Saga of Private Julius Cole." <u>Black World</u> 23 (Mar.
1974): 54-70. Rpt. as "Die Saga vom Gemeinen Julius
Cole." <u>Zwischenfall in Harlem</u>. Ed. Horst Ihde. Berlin:
Verlag Neues Leben, 1978. 276-298.

"The Saga of Private Julius Cole" is the first of Shockley's short stories to be placed in an anthology of
Afro-American writers translated into German. For the
reprint, Shockley was paid upon publication a one-time
fee of twenty marks per printed page (approximately
$7.83 per page). She did not receive the promised two
gratis copies of the anthology and comments that "German
publishers are bad about sending copies."

The story pivots on the theme of the universality of
man's inhumanity to man. It details the sad and heroic
plight of Julius Cole, a black private who fights
courageously on the front lines in Vietnam only to
come home and be greeted by marital infidelity, poor
employment opportunities, corrupt friends, and finally
death from black youths who mug him on a deserted
street. Shockley takes obvious delight in paying respect
to the black Vietnam veteran; for this reason, she
portrays him as a loving father, loyal husband, good
friend, and patriotic citizen. His encounters stateside
with hatred, distrust, deceit, and unfaithfulness ele-
vate him to martyr and render a sad commentary on
his mistreatment by those whose lives he fought to
save. The universality of his encounters gives the
story its permanence.

A37.   "Ah, the Young Black Poet." <u>New Letters</u> 41 (Winter
1974): 45-60.

This story gives considerable description to the incon-
siderate, vain actions of Melvin Frank Watts, a soph-
omore writer at Dubois College in Tetsee, Georgia.
A composite of many characters Shockley has observed,
Watts embodies the frustration and snobbishness peculiar
to writers. Taking three hours to scribble ten words
of gibberish, he habitually alienates himself from
his family. This alienation and his incapacity for
forward vision mark his self-destruction. Significantly,
his untimely demise heralds the early death of his
poetry that the publisher returns and the janitor
discards as trash when he cleans Watts' apartment for
rental again. The precipitous bad and good circumstances
in Watts' life symbolize the artist's dual nature as
destroyer and creator. His character contributes to
the theme -- the arrogant self-importance of young
writers too impatient for fame.

A38. "The More Things Change." Essence 8 (Oct. 1977): 78+.

This story is a critique of male chauvinism. It eval-
uates the actions of Curtis Edwards, III, a married
English professor and minister's son in the throes
of a mid-life crisis. His red bikini underwear, pot
smoking, and high priced Thunderbird with tape deck
and swivel bucket seats are symbols of his new self-
image. His extramarital affairs undertaken in defiance
of his Christian upbringing are emblematic of the double
standard society tolerates.

Central to Curtis' new life is the traditional belief
that a husband can do what he wants to in a marriage,
but the wife cannot. The major source of his irrational
anger is the discovery that his wife wants the divorce
he asks her for and that he is unable to determine
whether his extramarital affairs preceded hers. Because
his wife reacts contrary to his expectations -- "wives
were supposed to resist marital breakups" -- he goes
into a tailspin.

The story begins as it ends -- with Curtis and his
female student-lover parked in a secluded dark spot.
What transpires between this frame transforms him
into a reflective, cautious person. His change to conservatism contrasts sharply with the gaudiness of
his Thunderbird that "glistened like an ostentatious
orange insect against the warm spring skyline of night."
This contrast points to the absurdity of his extramarital affairs and the peculiarity of the mid-life
crisis. His hysterical laughter affirms this strange-
ness. The story's importance hinges on its discernment
of male psychology.

A39. "A Case of Telemania." Azalea 1 (Fall 1978): 1-5. Rpt.
in Lesbian Fiction: An Anthology. Ed. Elly Bulkin.
Watertown, MA.: Persephone P, 1981. 138-143.

"A Case of Telemania" is an interesting portrayal of
twenty-five-year-old Freda Delaney, a lonely black
intellectual who wants to identify with and relate
to other black women. She is a typical example of what
psychologists would refer to as an "oral character,"
her personality having been colored by the oral development stage at which she became fixated. Deriving
pleasure primarily in sucking, she draws her friends
into lengthy long distance telephone conversations,
smokes king-sized Winston cigarettes, and sips wine
between puffs. Her life is seemingly informed by the
insatiable desire to "take in" people, things, and
places. Her dislike for being alone and her longing
to receive are offset by her urge to give. Consistently,
she gives by way of mouth, an action which also manifests itself in her need to teach and converse with
black women. Always preoccupied with sustenance, she
harbors a suspicion that scarcity of black friends
and black places to teach will prevail.

Freda is an important character in Shockley's canon of fiction. She is one of the few black women characters struggling between two racial worlds to achieve person-hood. Unlike Shockley's male characters who remain in the black community and attempt to make inroads in mainstream America, Freda remains in white society and hopes for a place at a black college. She reveals that the black lesbian is as ostracized from the black community as the heterosexual black male is from the white. Similar to black male characters, she has diffi-culty proving her worth among whites; afterall, she has to fight "tooth and nail [at a white college] to teach a course in Afro-American history...." And similar to the male character who seeks the white woman to feed his ego, Freda takes in a white woman-lover to feed hers. Her circumstances crystallize the theme of the black lesbian's loneliness, insecurity, and uncertainties in heterosexual America.

A40.   "A Meeting of the Sapphic Daughters." Sinister Wisdom 9 (Spring 1979): 54-59. Rpt. in The Black and White of It. Tallahassee: Naiad P, 1980. 61-68.

"A Meeting of the Sapphic Daughters" examines tensions between two black lesbians and a group of white lesbians at an all-white Sapphic meeting. The tensions between the races embody the essence of hostility and racism and account, no doubt, for the absence of other black lesbians at a meeting where supposedly "all lesbians were welcome to attend." This story demonstrates the irony of human existence, wherein white lesbians who are excluded from the heterosexual world exclude blacks from their white lesbian world.

A41.   "Women in a Southern Time." Feminary 11 (1981): 45-56.

Set in the 1930's, this narrative repudiates the tradi-tional stereotypic images of Southern women, especially the submissive, dependent white woman and the God-fearing, matriarchal black maid. Each woman in this story has her own individuality: wealthy Tish Southerner marries, but has affairs with Monti Irving; Monti Irving, a northern-educated mannish-looking spinster, runs the local newspaper and moves to elect the black school principal to the town board; and Eula Mae, Tish Southerner's maid, diligently saves for a college ed-ucation, but becomes her white employer's lesbian lover and gives up the idea of attending school. The women's behaviors suggest a latent dissatisfaction with tradi-tional racism, sexism, and Southern conservatism. Iron-ically, the Southern community attributes their odd behavior to various reasons, including communism, over-work, and stupidity. The characters' actions are not always plausible; however, the story's importance lies in its advancement of the tabooed idea that lesbi-anism did exist in the conservative South in the 1930's among married and single, black and white women.

STORIES FIRST PUBLISHED IN SHORT STORY COLLECTION

A42.   "A Birthday Remembered." The Black and White of It.
        Tallahassee: Naiad P, 1980. 87-92. Rpt. in Between
        Mothers and Daughters. Ed. Susan Koppelman. Old West-
        bury, NY: Feminist P, 1985. 285-293.

        "A Birthday Remembered" is Shockley's first story about
        a straight person accepting a lesbian as a friend and
        individual. The visit of fourteen-year-old Tobie to
        Ellen Simms, celebrating her forty-fourth birthday,
        suggests a deep sense of respect for and kindness to
        her dead mother's lover. The visit closes the gap left
        by Tobie's mother's death, her father's claiming custody
        of her, and society's rejection of Ellen as lesbian.
        The plot unfolds through the reflections of Ellen on
        her birthday and gives another aspect of the aging,
        lonely lesbian. The effective omniscient narrator allows
        a glimpse of how three people's lives intersect and
        how each one is important to the other.

A43.   "Holly Craft Isn't Gay." The Black and White of It
        69-77.

        "Holly Craft Isn't Gay" sensitively reflects on the
        theme of self-denial. The theme centers in Holly Craft,
        a renowned concert singer who marries to quell the
        rumors that she is a lesbian. Her self-denial becomes
        the focal point of her existence as she struggles,
        during her husband's absence, to resist the advances
        of a former woman lover. The effect of this struggle
        reveals a curious contradiction in Holly Craft's ac-
        tions: she succumbs to her lover's embraces while ada-
        mantly saying, "I am not gay"; and she sleeps with
        her lover and plots to have her husband impregnate
        her so as to present to the public the image of a happy
        "straight family circle." Her repeating thrice that
        "this will be the last time" with her lover is an un-
        convincing resolution since her body's hunger is greater
        than her mental resolve. This story is dulled by the
        similar content presented in "Play It, But Don't Say
        It."

A44.   "Home to Meet the Folks." The Black and White of It
        51-59.

        Family rejection is the theme that winds through this
        story in which Roz Parrish, a black woman, takes Marge
        Hall, her white lover, home to meet her folks at Thanks-
        giving. The motif advances with various objections
        to the lesbian relationship presented to Roz by family
        members: the mother says, "It's against God's laws";
        Roz's sister-in-law views it as "a white trick for
        total black genocide"; and her brother regards it as
        something loathsome. The conflict is resolved when
        Roz denies her own family to be with Marge, an action
        that suggests misunderstanding of the lesbian experience

severely limits the lesbian's associations. The story
is important for its presentation of the negative manner
in which the black community regards lesbianism.

A45.   "Love Motion." The Black and White of It 93-95.

This is the only story in The Black and White of it
depicting a heterosexual affair. Positioned next to
the last of ten pieces, it seems misplaced. The shortest
of the ten, it could have easily served as a prologue
and bridge to the other stories with lesbian characters.
The story focuses on a brief, unpleasant, sexual inter-
course between a wife and her drunken, bad-smelling
husband. Unprepared for "his meat [which] felt like
a blunted sword in the open cavity of her," the wife
fantasizes making love to another woman.

The wife's fantasy is a rejection of the harsh, rape-
like, take-for-granted manner that too often accompanies
her marital copulations. But it is also her acceptance
of the fact that sexual expression with her husband
does not allow her "to know herself physically." The
story affirms the view that the love motion which should
occur in the copulative act sometimes becomes a sneer-
ingly disgusting exercise, particularly when the husband
"pulled out of her to flop like a dead fish over on
his back." Descriptive language and vivid details give
the story appeal.

A46.   "One More Saturday Night Around." The Black and White
of It 79-86.

"One More Saturday Night Around" has the spacial scope
reserved for a short story, but the third person narrator covers ten years in Marcia and Bethany's relationship. They are presented as unhappy, frustrated women
guided by lust for each other in their secret motel
meetings on Saturday nights. The narrator's stance
indicates that the women's Saturday night trysts will
cease when the chores of their "other" lives dissipate
lust (Marcia is married with two children, and Bethany
has someone at home waiting for her, too). Throughout
the story, the narrator undercuts the act of lust by
portraying the two women watching the clock and depart-
ing, despite the loneliness they experience in their
separation. Interest in this story wanes because it
does not differ essentially from others in the collection wherein lesbians deny themselves and encounter
a loneliness crisis.

A47.   "The Play." The Black and White of It 43-49.

The pain of sharing is the theme central to this story
about two lesbians. Robin represents commitment; Lynn,
her bisexual lover, freedom. The pain derived from
this dichotomy increases in proportion to Lynn's promiscuity and her tactless copulation with a macho man
in a car in Robin's presence. Robin's attempt to cool
the passions of the two by persistently blowing the
car horn proves futile. The unconfined cannot be re-

stricted; the world of the bisexual may allure, but it is not monogamous. The most Robin can hope for is Lynn's brief return to begin the cycle of hurt again. The story's interest resides in Robin, who disproves with her loyalty the general notion of lesbians' promiscuity.

A48. "Play It, But Don't Say It." The Black and White of It 25-42.

The story's title provides a clue to the major theme, denial. Denial for Mattie Bernice Brown, a distinguished political candidate, means keeping the public ignorant of her bisexual behavior, disallowing her lover to refer to their lesbian relationship, and, finally, ridding herself of her faithful lover. These conditions she insists upon with all the tenacity and aggressiveness of a male political figure seeking a successful candidacy. Since her successful public image depends on her unblemished personal life, growth requires making a public display of accoutrements acceptable to heterosexual society. Deferring to social restraints that enforce her lesbian denial, she negotiates connections between her personal experiences and those of the outside world. She may identify the heterosexual restraints that repress her, but she has not achieved the feminist perspective to confront and outmaneuver these inhibitions. As a political figure, Mattie Bernice Brown is less effective than the male figure she emulates. This story does not advance certain issues that are also presented in "Holly Craft Isn't Gay."

A49. "Spring into Autumn." The Black and White of It 1-23.

As a lesbian ages, the more lonely her existence marks the point of this story. Shockley creates her dominant impression through her choice of important details: the dreariness and harshness of the seasons, the desertion of a lover and friends, the weariness of body, and the general solitude that pervades the protagonist's home. The aging, lonely protagonist Penelope Bullock is made more aware of her plight by observing herself in the image of a woman seated on a bar stool: "She saw a woman her age with too-bright yellow hair swooping over a worn face, tense, smoking and drinking beer, trying not to seem too alone -- too lonely -- out of place." Observing the other woman changes Penelope Bullock's spring into autumn and causes internal trepidation not experienced before. Bullock's development is minimal, but her concerns as a middle-aged woman invite sympathy.

A50. "The World of Rosie Polk." Unpublished short story, 1974.

This story was originally written for Rollaway Productions, a black California-based film production company no longer in existence. It centers in Rosie Polk's world, narrowed by the parameters of an eastern shore of Virginia migrant camp, where the cycle of poverty and ignorance continues from one season to the next on the farm of wealthy white John Tilghman. Attention to details notably demonstrates the alarming discrepancy between the work Rosie and son perform and the benefits they reap: they thrive on baloney stew and grape sodas, live in a one-room shanty with no electricity, are prohibited from going into town, and perish the thought of every earning enough to buy store-bought clothes.

To Rosie's destitute, restricted existence, love comes to add a softening dimension seldom encountered in literature on migrant workers. Tired of leaving men and being left by men, Rosie and son find rest from a transitory existence in the secure life of Joe Louis Jackson, handyman for the Tilghman farm. The extent of Rosie's security with Jackson can be realized only in Jackson's few daily comforts that Rosie has been missing: Jackson lives in a two-room house with electricity, an ice box, sink, and stove; and he has fifty dollars in cash to pay off Rosie's debt to the boss. As deserving as Rosie is of a secure life with Jackson, her bettered circumstances do not speak for the hundreds of migrant workers perennially doomed to pick snap beans in a cycle of grinding poverty; yet her story as a migrant worker offers insight into the general conditions within a migrant camp.

SHORT STORY COLLECTION

A51. <u>The Black and White of It</u>. Tallahassee: Naiad P, 1980.

<u>The Black and White of It</u> is generally considered the first published short story collection about lesbians written by a black woman. Shockley began the collection in the 1960's and submitted it to several publishers. Diana Press offered to published it but had a financial setback in 1978; Shockley then sent the collection to The Naiad Press. The collection consists of ten stories, three of which do not refer to racial identity. The title, therefore, does not totally refer to ethnic backgrounds, but rather to the good and bad situations all the women characters find themselves in.

Basically, a one-plot pattern dominates this collection about tenuous, fragile lesbian relationships in hetero-sexual, male dominated communities. The plot pattern progresses from the lesbian's fear of discovery, to separation of lovers, to the deep longing for woman-bonding relations. Variations within this plot pattern relieve the collection from tedium. Some mixed elements include a lover's induced alteration to her affair ("The Play"), black lesbians ostracized by white les-bians ("A Meeting of the Sapphic Daughters"), inter-racial lovers rising above familial ostracism ("Home to Meet the Folks"), and a mother having clandestine relations with a past lover ("One More Saturday Night Around"). Such variations cut across the typical rela-tionships where one of the partners experiences extreme loneliness or fear. Overall, this type of plot pattern, even with mixed elements, is designed to produce the vision that society's insensitiveness to lesbians offers too few opportunities for their self-expression and thus casts them in a pale from which it is difficult to extricate themselves.

Through the use of strategically placed images, Shockley effectively clarifies the rigidness of the environment surrounding lesbian characters. Overwhelmingly, these images nullify the open, vibrant, comfortable expecta-tions of love and insist on isolation, decay, and diffi-culty. The images occur at the beginning of a relation-ship, when expectation is high, and at the severing point, when hopes are dashed. While there are descrip-tions of food ("wilted head of lettuce"), household objects ("the phone went dead"), and pavement ("rough-tongued street"), most of the tactile images charac-terize the weather. The "hovering grayness" of January, "switchblade flash of lightning," foot-clinging white snow, biting bleak and cold weather "representing February's dung" -- all knot together as a societal conspiracy to annihilate the lesbian relationship. The bleak reality in these stories is a unifying thread tightening the plot structure and deepening the les-bian's undesirable position in hetereosexual, Christian America.

Critical responses to <u>The Black and White of It</u>,
although mixed, have been favorable. The collection
has been praised for its candid treatment of homophobia,
racism, and myth breaking; and it has been viewed as
an important work in lesbian fiction. The adverse criticism focuses on limited character development and
the perenially restricted and negative world in which
the lesbian characters find themselves. Whatever limita-
tion the characters may have might be attributed to
Shockley's heterosexual vision in developing them;
this perspective is an interaction of her sentiments
and societal pressures restricting lesbian development.

NOVELS

A52.   Loving Her. New York: Bobbs-Merrill, 1974. New York: Avon, 1978.

Loving Her is Shockley's third novel but the first to be published. It was titled A Love So Bold until editors at Bobbs-Merrill, to Shockley's dissatisfaction, changed the title to Loving Her. The Avon paperback edition, which originally sold for $1.75 per copy in 1978, appeared on the Christopher Street Best Seller List in that magazine's December 1978 issue. The Best Seller List for Christopher Street "is compiled from monthly sales reports received from Giovanni's Room in Philadelphia, Lambda Rising in Washington, DC, the Oscar Wilde Memorial Bookstore in New York, and the Walt Whitman Bookstore in San Francisco."

In this work, more than in any other, Shockley explores the myth of the black prince charming in the character of Jerome Lee Davis, husband to Renay, the protagonist. "Big and brown and handsome with stiff curly hair and flashing dark eyes," Jerome fits every girl's dream (except Renay's) of handsome prince charming. That he is the star football player at a Kentucky college adds to his personal charm. Cracks in the myth appear when he pursues Renay, before marriage, for the challenge, rather than for sincerity. His pursuit is macho and common: "he bombarded the dormitory with telephone calls for her, chased her and cajoled her." His date with her to his spring fraternity dance is not a prologue to a happy life thereafter, but an introduction into a brutal and hellish existence made more unbearable by Jerome's seriously flawed personality. Guilty of drunkenness, rape, and homicide, Jerome falls short of the average woman's expectations of such a good-looking man.

The prince charming myth forms a backdrop to and an explanation for the lesbian life-style Renay chooses for herself. Such a life-style enables one to view the lesbian relationship as an alternate for those women disappointed by heterosexual love. Glaring contrasts between Jerome and Terry, Renay's white woman-lover, solicit understanding of, but not necessarily agreement with, Renay's change. Terry's inordinate care, sincerity, and generosity emphasize the ideal qualities women expect the prince charming character to possess; and the absence of these characteristics looms large in the eyes of the mistreated mate. One must consider, however, that no one is totally good (as Terry is) or totally bad (as Jerome is). Renay's being swept away by mannish Terry makes her as much a victim of the prince charming myth as her college girlfriends, agog over Jerome.

Whereas Loving Her merits attention for its treatment of the prince charming myth from a black perspective,

critiques of the novel have been mostly negative. These
cite excessive propaganda, faulty plot structure, poor
literary style, inaccurate characterization, and dis-
regard for time relevance. All are correct. The first
published novel about black lesbianism by a black woman,
Shockley has turned the literary soil for others to
plant.

A53.   Say Jesus and Come to Me. New York: Avon, 1982.

Say Jesus and Come to Me was originally intended to
be the first story in The Black and White of It, but
mainstream publishers at that time wanted a novel.
Despite its unconventional subject matter, Say Jesus
and Come to Me was quickly marketed. Shockley's agent
"sold it at the first shot to Avon." This method dif-
fered considerably from that relating to Loving Her,
which Shockley sent to a multitude of publishers for
years and finally got it accepted by Bobbs-Merrill,
she admits, "because a straight, black male editor
recognized my name and liked the book." Both novels
are currently out of print.

Say Jesus and Come to Me is a comically intense satire
burlesquing homophobia in the black church. The effec-
tiveness of the attack resides primarily in juxtaposing
Reverend Myrtle Black, the lesbian protagonist, with
her heterosexual male counterpart whom she imitates.
Both take delight in gender superiority: Reverend Black
brags that she is "God's gift to church and womankind";
Reverend Cross exaggerates his heterosexual male importance by excluding homosexuals from his church. Both
use the same tactics of saving souls and administering
to the sexual needs of female parishioners: Reverend
Black mesmerizes latent lesbians during the altar call,
steadily grinds her hips into theirs, and fervently
cries out, "Say Jesus and come to me"; one male counterpart fondles little girls behind the altar, grieves
his wife with adulterous acts, and asks his congregation
if there is another soul to come to Christ. The placement of Reverend Black alongside the black male minister
accentuates the moral shabbiness of both and demotes
them to irresponsible pawns in an unholy racket. The
wonder of it all, Shockley seems to say, is that there
is always the enrapt congregation to curry the favor
of and egg on the man of the cloth.

Reverend Black's colorful, excessively fringed robe
mocks the tattered black habit of her male counterpart,
while both frocks veil the deficiencies of the self-
serving, intolerant, and morally disintegrating corpus
within. For her own survival, Reverend Black connivingly
operates to deconstruct patriarchal Christianity,
while her male counterpart functions deceitfully to
preserve it for the same reason. The irreparable rift
between the two factions widens more when the church,
representing tolerance, justice, and love, cannot bind
the rivaling forces. The manifestation of the church's
impotence gives Shockley's fullest statement yet of

her disillusionment with that homophobic black institution.

The satire advances with revealing language. The play
on words, especially proper names, belittles. Reverend
Cross's surname appropriately suggests a morbidly ag-
gressive and ill-tempered pastor, rather than Christ's
humble follower dispensing a universal love for mankind.
And Reverend Black's maiden name points up her improper
manipulation of language to undermine the sanctity
of patriarchal Christianity. She yokes the sacred and
profane: to her lover before the sexual act, she says,
"Close your eyes, darling,... and let me enter the
pearly gates." Such cliches as "scare the bejesus out
of her" and "pimping for Jesus" also affront Christian
terminology. All in all, there is no sense of redemption
in the language; Shockley did not intend for there
to be any.

Obviously, the main attack is on the church arena;
however, Shockley had a larger ambition. She writes:
"I wanted to bring out the homophobic hypocrisy of
the black church, which is filled to the pulpit with
closet gays and lesbians from all walks of life....I
wanted to expose the conservatism and snobbishness
of the black middle class and academicians which I
see all the time; black male oppression of women, the
superior attitudes and opportunism of some white women
towards black women in the women's liberation movement,
and even touch on the local country music scene" (unpublished letter to author). Shockley's ambition is
commendable, but her aim is short-circuited in this
novel which does contain structural flaws. Episodes
meander and dangle, often consisting of more polemics
than action; topics are unevenly weighted; some speeches
are too long; digs at prominent black idols (MLK and
Bobby Blane) are hurried; and some coincidences stretch
plausibility. Toward the end of the novel, the third
person narrator introduces characters only peripherally
connected to Reverend Black's goal.

Yet in this thickly plotted novel, in this maze of
satiric targets, glows a distinctly religious iconoclasm
never before revealed with such intensity in the fiction of black American women. Behind this iconoclasm
stands Shockley, who remains unperturbed about her
readers' dislike for her unconventionality: "There
will always be [more] who dislike the theme than like
it. That doesn't bother me. I shall forever be considered a minor writer anyhow."

A54. Not to be Alone. Unpublished novel, ca. 1950.

This is Shockley's first novel, written when she was
in her twenties. Approximately 189 pages in length,
it depicts middle-class blacks during World War II.
The setting is Louisville, Kentucky.

A55. A World of Lonely Strangers. Unpublished novel, ca.
       1960.

       Shockley's second novel, it is the first with a lesbian
       theme. Her literary agent had difficulty marketing
       it because of its content. It contains 184 pages;
       Loving Her grew out of it.

II.
NONFICTION WRITTEN BY ANN ALLEN SHOCKLEY

NEWSPAPER COLUMNS

Louisville Defender

"Mostly Teen Talk" is the first newspaper column Ann Allen Shockley wrote. The following three issues, badly frayed and brittle, she kept in her scrapbook. The last two entries have no precise date and page number.

1945

A56.   7 July 1945: 3. A note of the unbearable heat precedes teen announcements of a friend being honorably discharged from the Army, a Brownie Girl Scout Troop program, and other miscellaneous items. Attention to detail and a conversational style are evident in this early column. It appears with an accompanying photograph of Shockley.

A57.   July 1945: N. pag. This column focuses on local parties, returning servicemen, Friskites working summer jobs in other cities, and vacationing guests.

A58.   July 1945: N. pag. The columnist announces that this is the last time she will write this column and that she "will deviate from the usual trend of this column and write at random." She describes a first day in the life of a high schooler back from vacation, new dress fads, and men returning from overseas.

Fisk University Herald

"Duffy's Corner" is the column Shockley wrote, while a student at Fisk University, in Fisk University Herald. It concerns duffers who infract Emily Post's rules

of etiquette. Material for the column was collected
from campus scenes and personages.

1945

A59. Mar. 1945: 11. Shockley documents a particular case
whereby a very tall male poorly escorted a Fisk University woman to a dance in Jubilee Hall. To gain her
composure, the young woman entered Meharry Hospital
for a rest on the day after the dance. The male's inane
behavior and clumsiness are treated humorously. Shockley
seems preoccupied with pointing up behavioral differ-
ences between the sexes.

A60. Apr. 1945: 15+. With a short story frame, this entry
plots the actions of a kangaroo court established after
a student riot in Jubilee Hall. Court proceedings dis-
close the students' typical attack on campus cafeteria
food: one wounded student fell unconscious after he
was hit on the head with a piece of Fisk toast. The
one-woman jury overlooks the poor cafeteria food, finds
the students guilty, and sentences them "to four long
weeks of hard reading of [Emily Post] in the library."

Federalsburg Times

Shockley called her column in this paper "Ebony Topics";
it presents her personal opinions about various subjects
and announces local community affairs. The following
quotation from the newspaper's editor precedes the
first entry: "For many years the only news of the
colored people of this community published in The Times
was of the sensational type, such as crimes, etc.
Realizing that this is unfair to our many friends and
readers of the Negro race, we are happy to inaugurate
this column, which we hope will be a permanent feature."
The only surviving copy of the 1949 issues of this
paper is located in the Maryland Room at the Enoch
Pratt Free Library in Baltimore, Maryland. Because
of the paper's brittleness and general state of decay
(there are no current plans to bind it), I have quoted
Shockley extensively on some important issues to preserve her thoughts as a young writer.

1949

A61. 7 Jan. 1949: 7. Shockley announces a birth in the community, welcomes holiday visitors, and makes known
the 1949 elected officers for the local NAACP chapter.

A62. 14 Jan. 1949: 3. Local church affairs are mentioned.
Shockley travelled with others to Philadelphia to see
the mummer's parade, but it had been postponed.

A63. 21 Jan. 1949: 8. The inauguration week of President
Truman is "a week of heavenly bliss for some and dis-
appointment for others." Without further comment on
Truman's induction, Shockley announces the installation

of new officers at the local NAACP chapter.

A64.   11 Feb. 1949: 2. In observance of Negro History Week, Shockley writes: "Perhaps there will be a time when no particular week will be needed to honor and bring to the attention of school children these men and women who have aided in the molding of the nation, but their achievements integrated in history as Americans and not as gens of color [sic]."

A65.   18 Feb. 1949: 7. This column praises a recent editorial appearing in the <u>Journal of Negro Education</u> attacking a drive by southerners to establish regional school systems. "The plan," posits Shockley, "that was conceived in a conference held in Savannah, Georgia, is a feeble defense against the growing tendency towards the inevitable -- equality in the educational realm which will automatically aid the nation in improving the educational standards."

A66.   4 Mar. 1949: 8. The national chapter of the NAACP set aside last Sunday as a day on which religious leaders of all denominations throughout the nation condemned intolerance.

A67.   11 Mar. 1949: 7. While another season has arrived, Shockley reflects that "it seemed only yesterday that the editor christened this column," and reminds local citizens not to let the Red Cross Fund drive pass without their contributing donations.

A68.   1 Apr. 1949: 7. This issue contains one of Shockley's early defenses for the rights of women. After commenting on "Moscow's recent boisterous remarks concerning [American] women as being subservient to men which led many of them to drink," she admonishes people of Moscow "to delve a little more deeply into the subject...[and] read Mary Beard's <u>Woman as a Force in History</u> [where they can] view the work of American women who fought for suffrage and equal rights."

A69.   8 Apr. 1949: 10. The Anderson college choir from Anderson, Indiana, presented an enjoyable musical program at the local Church of God. Shockley comments that "The [racially] mixed choir does not only show its musical ability, but points out to those geographic areas that are still deep in the slough of cynicalism [sic] that non-segregated schools are an added spoke in the wheel of promoting brotherhood."

A70.   22 Apr. 1949: 9. Gaity and solemnity are the twin emotions accompanying Easter. Too often this occasion is looked upon "as merely a holiday and time to deck ourselves in new attire," when we should "always keep in mind all the year what is the real significance of Easter."

A71.   29 Apr. 1949: 10. Shockley views with regret W.E.B. DuBois' aligning himself with extremist Paul Robeson at the World Peace Conference. She speculates: "DuBois

in his alliance, has automatically thrown his greatly
needed talents and efforts in promoting social justice
away, for in the present role of communist, there is
little he can do, aside from loud emotional bombasting,
to continue the work that he has previously been praised
[for]." She warns other leaders not to become "too
impatient and disgusted with the signs of the times
today and desert to the ranks of leftism where their
abilities will be of no avail."

A72. 6 May 1949: 9. Shockley reports on the twenty-first
annual meeting of the Maryland Congress of Parent-
Teacher Association, held in Cambridge, Maryland. It
had as its theme "Fundamental Needs in the Training
of American Youth." The key issue was the responsibilities of the home, school, and community in training
youth.

A73. 13 May 1949: 9. Shockley's Mother's Day tribute to
mother is: "Instead of accepting what she does at face
value, try to hang up the motto in your thoughts that
everyday is Mother's Day and make it bright for her."

A74. 20 May 1949: 4. The sudden twists in May's weather
prompt Shockley to disbelieve the male adage, "Women
are as changeable as the weather."

A75. 3 June 1949: 2. Shockley records that the ninth annual
Maryland State Conference of the NAACP branches convened
in Baltimore, Saturday, May 21, 1949, at Sharp Street
Methodist Church. The speakers included Thurgood Mar-
shall, Special Counsel for the NAACP; Clarence Mitchell,
National Labor Secretary; and Furnam Templeton, Associate Director of Baltimore Housing Authority. Turning
to another subject, Shockley stresses Memorial Day
as a time for remembering: "Even though the physical
form may have disintegrated into an abyss of nothing-
ness, we can put a wreath on a remembrance of those
we love."

A76. 10 June 1949: 2. Announcements are made of commencement
dates and closings of local schools for the summer.

A77. 1 July 1949: 7. The Caroline County branch of the NAACP
had a parade celebrating the fortieth anniversary of
the organization and the terminating of the Miss Caroline County Contest. Miss Caroline County, a Denton
resident, was crowned at Zion Methodist Church after
the parade.

A78. 15 July 1949: 10. The arrival and passing of Independence Day allow many to reflect on Jefferson's speech
regarding life, liberty, and the pursuit of happiness.
Shockley hopes that "we can look forward to the times
when the euphonious words of Jefferson will not only
be something we quote in speeches and [at] banquets
and [on] holidays, and teach parrot-like to school
children, but will be a realistic picture of American

life where all, regardless of race or religion, are
looked upon as having those inalienable rights."

A79. 22 July 1949: 9. Federalsburg Times celebrates
its twentieth anniversary. Shockley salutes the paper
"for reporting accurately and objectively the news
and being a mouth organ for the voices of the people."
She views the newspaper in general as "a vehicle of
expression, a communicator with the world," and
"a traffic officer that regulates the political drivers
in national affairs."

A80. 5 Aug. 1949: 2. The Caroline County branch of the NAACP
sponsored a summer bus excursion to Atlantic City's
beach, and the Sunday School Department of Zion Methodist Church sponsored one to Sparrow's Beach in Maryland.

A81. 12 Aug. 1949: 2. Shockley makes announcements of local
weddings, vacations, and in-town visitors.

A82. 16 Sept. 1949: 5. Shockley bids farewell to her readers;
she plans to reside in Delaware with her husband. She
makes an important comparison between writing this
column and writing short stories: "I watch each character come to life and breathe and go in the direction
I want...." She concludes by thanking the editor "for
being so cooperative when I approached him with the
idea of this type of column in the interest of the
minority group which is a faithful reader of The Times."

Bridgeville News

"Ebony Topics" is the title of Shockley's column that
appeared in Bridgeville News; similar to her column
for Federalsburg Times, she writes of various
issues, social, political, and otherwise. The column
appeared from November 1950 until March 1954 and is
still readable in issues of Bridgeville News, housed
at the five-room public library in Bridgeville, Delaware. 1950 and 1951 issues of this newspaper are stacked
in inverted order between two large pieces of cardboard
held together by screws and nuts; subsequent issues
are bound. When Shockley's column contains non-local
news and local news, I have emphasized the former,
which appears to have more historical value than the
latter.

1950

A83. 3 Nov. 1950: 5. Shockley introduces "Ebony Topics"
as "a column devoted to social activities, news, and
views of interest to the colored people of Bridgeville."
She then gives recognition to friends and relatives

serving in the Korean War, announces the thirty-second
annual convention of the Delaware State Education
Association, and reminds her readership to send news
of interest to her that they would like to have published.

A84.   24 Nov. 1950: 4. Shockley posits that Armistice Day,
which heralded the end of World War I, has a different
meaning for the younger generation than it has for
those older persons who have lost loved ones in the
war. To the former, it means "only something to be
studied in history books"; for the latter, it means
comparing the "second war with the first and fervently
[praying] that the final outcome of these two gigantic
struggles whose repercussions still have not terminated
will end in peace." Other local news follows.

A85.   1 Dec. 1950: 6. Footbal games and Thanksgiving dinners
are at the center of this week's news.

A86.   8 Dec. 1950: 6. The Delaware State College Sussex County
Alumni Association gets the spotlight for the week.
The Association sponsored a musical tea for the benefit
of the College's Athletic Fund, and the Association's
President is congratulated for his work in awarding
scholarships and generally helping the College with
its many undertakings.

A87.   15 Dec. 1950: 4. Tribute is paid to Human Rights Day,
Dec. 10th, and the columnist reminds readers that "Now
more than ever when our country along with those of
the UN are engaged in one of the bloodiest battles
in modern times, we should remember and bring to mind
the human goals set forth in the Declaration, for they
are what we as a free nation are trying to preserve
and strive for as a standard to others." Shockley calls
attention to the recent awarding of the Nobel Peace
Prize to Dr. Ralph Bunche in Oslo, Norway. She regards
this event "an illustration of our country as a dynamic
exponent of freedom."

A88.   22 Dec. 1950: 7. With the approaching holidays, readers
are reminded to "reserve a space in [their] thoughts
for [Christ]." Local holiday preparations, guests,
and a New Year's Eve Watch Meeting Service are an-
nounced. The columnist extends to all " a merry Christmas and a happy new year."

A89.   29 Dec. 1950: 6. A yuletide calendar of dinners, parties, and other festive affairs dominates this week's
news.

1951

A90.   5 Jan. 1951: 5. The columnist recapitulates the events
of the previous year in which "Negroes excelled in

their respective fields." She cites Ralph Bunche's receiving the Nobel Peace Prize and Althea Gibson's becoming the first black to play tennis at Forest Hills. The columnist then reports that "we need to look ahead and hope that this embryo of 1951 will burst forth with newer and fresher progress for the race."

A91. 12 Jan. 1950: 8. In observance of George Washington Carver Week, the Phillis Wheatley School held a Carver Day Program during which the life and work of the ex-slave were reviewed. Other local news follows.

A92. 19 Jan. 1951: 8. Dominating the local news this week is the return of Harry Douglas to Bridgeville, his hometown, for a brief visit with his family. Leader of the famous musical quintet Deep River Boys, Douglas will be appearing for engagements in Montreal, Canada; New York; and Philadelphia. His musical group started when he was a student at Hampton Institute in Hampton, Virginia, more than fifteen years ago.

A93. 26 Jan. 1951: 5. Of special note is that Salesium Catholic High School in Wilmington, Delaware, has opened its doors to blacks. This columnist reminds us that it is time to heed the words of the school's rector who says, "It's a case of reaching a point of either stopping the preaching of democracy or starting to practice it." Other local news includes visits, guests, dinners, and church services.

A94. 2 Feb. 1951: 5. February 1st was Freedom Day, once set aside to observe the final adoption of the four-teenth and fifteenth amendments. These two amendments are of the utmost importance in the history of our country, and persons of all races, according to Shock-ley, "should stop to commemorate the freedom guaranteed to them as citizens."

A95. 9 Feb. 1951: 4. Among the local news are a baby shower, out-of-town visits, and the forthcoming television appearance of Harry Douglas and his Deep River Boys.

A96. 23 Feb. 1951: 4. Following a notice of the observance of Brotherhood Week are local notices of weekend guests, a farewell party, and a special program at Trinity Methodist Church.

A97. 9 Mar. 1951: 5. A surprised birthday party for a local resident, notice of the sick and shut-in, and the Phillis Wheatley's faculty attending an educational conference at the University of Delaware are the major news items.

A98. 16 Mar. 1951: 5. Announcements include travel, visits, the Red Cross Drive, and Jason High School's completion of a survey relating to its instituting a guidance training program.

A99.   30 Mar. 1951: 5. Women's Easter attire and family
        visits highlight this week's news.

A100.   6 Apr. 1951: 5. The local news includes preparations
        for the Annual Methodist Conference, a program fea-
        turing the Ideal Gospel Singers and the famous Chris-
        tianaires of Baltimore, a local Jackson family at-
        tending a fifth generation family reunion in Wil-
        mington, other visits, and guests.

A101.   20 Apr. 1951: 5. News includes Dr. Ralph Bunche's
        presenting Joseph Mankiewicz with an academy award
        for the best motion picture of the year, All about
        Eve. This act, writes Shockley, marks Dr. Bunche as
        "the first colored person to ever make such a presen-
        tation." Other news includes dinner guests and motoring
        trips.

A102.   27 Apr. 1951: 5. Foremost in the news is an argument
        among alumni, spectators, and students regarding what
        should be done with Delaware State College since
        Negroes are now allowed to attend the University of
        Delaware. The Essex County Alumni Association met
        to discuss the issue and concluded that the College
        should remain open but "on an accredited basis mainly
        because of economic reasons and educational back-
        grounds [of the students]". Other news includes back-
        ground information on the formation of the Bridgeville
        American Legion Post, a Canasta and television party,
        and a birthday party.

A103.   11 May 1951: 5. Shockley announces that with the ar-
        rival of Dr. Frederick Smith, a graduate of Prairie
        View College and the University of Michigan, Delaware
        "now has a Negro veterinarian." Other local news
        follows.

A104.   25 May 1951: 7. The Phillis Wheatley School's PTA
        held its final meeting for the year, during which
        officers were reelected and committees reinstated.
        Other local news includes a christening, a dinner,
        and a party.

A105.   1 June 1951: 4. The major news includes the Bridgeville
        Boys Scouts' attending the Annual Camporee at Trappe
        Pond, Delaware.

A106.   15 June 1951: 5. News includes the Phillis Wheatley
        School's commencement and the columnist's attending
        a local wedding.

A107.   13 July 1951: 4. This column was received too late
        to be printed last week. It notes the passing of Inde-
        pendence Day, cites the famous words of Thomas Jeffer-
        son -- "All men are created equal..." -- and sug-
        gests that these words "will soon be the basis for
        an unchaotic and democratic world."

A108. 20 July 1951: 8. The Sparrow's Beach outing, sponsored
       by the Delaware State College Alumni Association,
       highlights this week's news. The columnist and her
       family attended.

A109. 27 July 1951: 8. A local wedding, beach trips, and
       guests highlight this week's news.

A110. 3 Aug. 1951: 5. Local news includes a wedding and
       out-of-town visits.

A111. 31 Aug. 1951: 4. This column has not appeared for
       several weeks because the columnist has been vaca-
       tioning in Louisville, Kentucky. Dominating the news
       is Ida Douglas, who has become an added feature to
       the new WJWL radio station in Georgetown. She can
       be heard singing and playing the lastest hit songs
       weekdays at 3:05 p.m. Other local news follows.

A112. 7 Sept. 1951: 5. Local school teachers are welcomed
       back for the beginning of the school year, and an-
       nouncements are given of holiday visits, a wedding,
       and a wiener roast.

A113. 14 Sept. 1951: 8. Shockley cites the Japanese Peace
       Conference as an important event in world history
       and notes that many in Bridgeville will view it on
       their local television stations. Church news dominates
       other local news.

A114. 21 Sept. 1951: 5. Harry Douglas and his famed Deep
       River Boys performed at the London Palladium in England
       and scored popularity points by recording a special
       birthday greeting to Her Royal Highness, Princess
       Margaret. The message begins, "Your Royal Highness,
       Princess Margaret, We the Deep River Boys, as ambas-
       sadors of song representing fifteen million American
       Negroes, salute you on this, your 21st birthday."
       This musical group is "rated in the first five leading
       entertainment attractions throughout England."

A115. 5 Oct. 1951: 4. Bridgeville baseball fans are gather-
       ing at the homes of television owners to watch the
       world series. Other local baseball fans have just
       returned from Philadelphia after viewing the game
       between the Brooklyn Dodgers and Phillies and "the
       history making playing of Jackie Robinson."

A116. 12 Oct. 1951: 8. Along with other local news is a
       tribute paid to Ida Douglas, a local up-and-coming
       pianist. Playing the piano since the age of ten, Miss
       Douglas has performed for the Salisbury and Seaford
       radio stations, entertained at Seaford Sussex Grill,
       and performed with a combo at Delaware State College,
       where she is a student.

A117. 19 Oct. 1951: 5. Local news includes the annual PTA
       membership drive, the meeting of the Sussex County
       Delaware State College Alumni Association at the home

of its president in Milford, dinners, and teas.

A118.   26 Oct. 1951: 5. In observance of United Nations Week,
        the Phillis Wheatley School presented a program with
        special emphasis placed on Mrs. Edith Sampson, Negro
        lawyer and alternate delegate to the United Nations.
        Other announcements include a reception, memorial
        services, and a teachers' conference.

A119.   2 Nov. 1951: 5. Television viewers expressed sadness
        and gladness as they watched Rocky Marciano's victory
        over ex-champ Joe Louis. Of one of the best boxing
        champions in the world, Shockley writes, "Old Joe
        may have died in the ring but he will never fade away
        in the hearts of the world." Other local news in-
        cludes teachers' attending the Annual Delaware State
        Education Association Convention, local citizens visit-
        ing out-of-town, and the Delaware State College Alum-
        ni Association sponsoring a raffle to raise funds
        for a scholarship to be given to a worthy student.

A120.   9 Nov. 1951: 8. The Women's Auxiliary of the Paskins
        American Legion Post gave a supper at Mt. Calvary
        Methodist Church on Friday night. Proceeds from the
        supper will aid the Auxiliary's plans to "adopt" a
        child at the Governor Bacon Health Center; that is,
        the organization will make monthly donations to an
        unfortunate child at the Center.

A121.   16 Nov. 1951: 5. Phillis Wheatley School observes
        American Education Week; it presented at its Tuesday
        night PTA meeting a skit called "The School Yesterday
        and Today." Members of the local William Paskins
        American Legion Post 24 observed Armistice Day by
        visiting veterans in the VA Hospital Brack-Ex near
        Wilmington. Other local news includes the passing
        of Mrs. Jamsie Douglas, the mother of Harry Douglas,
        leader of the renowned Deep River Boys.

A122.   23 Nov. 1951: 5. Harry Douglas has just returned from
        his third annual British tour with his Deep River
        Boys. Other news includes Delaware State College's
        homecoming activities, dinner, and a funeral.

A123.   30 Nov. 1951: 4. The appearance of Janet Collins in
        the ballet scene of "Aida" at New York's Metropolitan
        Opera House "marks the first time a Negro has ever
        performed on that stage." Announcements of local
        dinners and visits follow.

A124.   14 Dec. 1951: 6. The spring-like weather has not
        deterred the Ladies Auxiliary of American Legion Post
        24 from distributing Christmas baskets to the needy.
        Among other announcements is the annual Christmas
        program at the Phillis Wheatley School, where two
        plays entitled "It Is More Blesed" and "What Is Christ-
        mas?" will be presented.

A125.   28 Dec. 1951: 1. This column was too late to be printed
        the previous week. Travel plans of some residents
        are given, and holiday cheer is extended to all.

                                1952

A126.   11 Jan. 1952: 5. The local Phillis Wheatley School
        celebrated the birthday of the late scientist George
        Washington Carver by presenting a special program,
        during which students read papers and poems.

A127.   25 Jan. 1952: 4. Local news includes the annual March
        of Dimes drive, the Boy Scouts Leaders Training meet-
        ing, the Sussex County Alumni Association of Delaware
        meeting, and out-of-town guests.

A128.   1 Feb. 1952: 5. Shockley reports that owing to the
        chaos in the world, the national commanders of the
        American Legion have asked all legionnaires and auxil-
        iaries to cooperate in a Go-to-Church Sunday cele-
        bration. The William Paskins American Legion Post
        in Bridgeville will attend the local Mt. Cavalry
        Methodist Church.

A129.   8 Feb. 1952: 5. Boy Scouts of America, founded February
        8, 1910, celebrates its forty-second anniversary the
        week of February 6th to 12th. The intent of the pro-
        gram is to build the minds and bodies of its members.

A130.   15 Feb. 1952: 8. Shockley notes a double reason for
        blacks' celebrating February 12th: Negro History Week
        was founded by the late black historian Carter G.
        Woodson, February 12, 1926; and Abraham Lincoln, the
        slave emancipator, was born February 12th.

A131.   22 Feb. 1952: 8. Paying tribute to Brotherhood Week,
        Shockley writes: "One world can only be achieved by
        knowing the inner value and worth of men accepting
        all as brothers." She concludes with statements on
        the meaning of brotherhood given by local residents.

A132.   29 Feb. 1952: 8. The local PTA of the Phillis Wheatley
        School gave a membership tea. For the year 1951-1952,
        there were 162 members.

A133.   7 Mar. 1952: 5. Shockley appeals to all to donate
        to the Red Cross campaign. Other local news focuses
        on the sick and shut in, concerts, and meetings.

A134.   21 Mar. 1952: 8. A top musical hit, "The Wheel of
        Fortune," was composed by George Weiss and Benny
        Benjamin, a black. Other hits accredited to this team
        are "I Ran All the Way Home," "These Things I Offer
        You," and "To Think You've Chosen Me." Other news
        includes baseball games, traveling, and the sick and
        shut in.

A135.   4 Apr. 1952: 2 . The news reports the sixth annual
        State Convention of the Delaware Association of the
        New Homemakers of America, Youth Day at Mt. Calvary
        Methodist Church, and out-of-town guests.

A136.   11 Apr. 1952: 4. Shockley mentions interest is high
        in the recent courageous decision of Chancellor Seitz
        regarding admission of black students to white schools
        in Claymont and Hockessin. She believes well-equipped
        schools are necessary for better prepared and socially
        responsible citizens.

A137.   25 Apr. 1952: 6. Shockley makes a tribute to spring.

A138.   2 May 1952: 5. It was approximately two years ago
        on May 1st when Gwendolyn Brooks, the first black,
        won the Pulitzer Prize for her volume of poems Annie
        Allen. More recently, Mary Elizabeth Vroman, author
        of short story "See How They Run," which appeared
        in Ladies Home Journal and which is being made into
        a movie, is the first black woman to be admitted to
        the Screen Writers Guild. Shockley views these as
        considerable accomplishments.

A139.   9 May 1952: 5. The choice of Mrs. Toy Len Goon of
        Portland, Maine, as "American Mother of 1952" is "a
        challenge and inspiration to the younger mothers of
        this nation." A native of China, Mrs. Goon operates
        a laundry, while rearing and educating eight children.
        To mothers everywhere she offers the challenge that
        "regardless of race, color, or creed, there exists
        the fundamental opportunity of surmounting all ob-
        structions to obtain goals...." Other news follows.

A140.   16 May 1952: 6. For the first time in the Wilmington
        Bowling Association, blacks were recently permitted
        to participate in the city championship. The black
        entrants won first prize in the two events and broke
        the tournament record. Shockley also makes a tribute
        to mother in honor of Mother's Day.

A141.   23 May 1952: 2. The grand opening of the Northwest
        Dover Heights Project in Dover was held Sunday. The
        housing project, offering improved housing facilities
        to blacks in lower Delaware, is the dream of Harley
        F. Taylor, praised by the governor "for his foresight-
        edness and leadership in race relations."

A142.   6 June 1952: 6. In honor of those who died in the
        Civil War, the local William Paskins American Legion
        Post held a very impressive service at Mt. Calvary
        Methodist Church on Memorial Day. Shockley includes
        the local schools' June commencement calendar.

A143.   13 June 1952: 2. Shockley recognizes June 14th as the
        175th anniversary of the flag of the United States
        and gives its symbolic meanings. Other news includes
        commencement exercises at Phillis Wheatley School

and Frederick Douglass School and a reminder to remember Dad on Father's Day.

A144.   20 June 1952: 5. Since the awarding of the Spingarn Medal in 1913, such persons as Marian Anderson, Richard Wright, and Walter White have received the honor. This year, the thirty-seventh award posthumously went to Harry T. Moore, Florida NAACP leader, for his outstanding fight for civil rights in Florida. Moore was killed at home by a bomb explosion during the Christmas season.

A145.   27 June 1952: 6. Shockley refers to an article on race relations appearing in the June issue of <u>Ladies Home Journal</u>, announces the last meeting of the year for the Ladies Auxiliary of the Volunteer Fire Company, and mentions those local persons who attended the national PTA meeting at West Virginia State College Institute.

A146.   4 July 1952: 3. Shockley refers to Thomas Jefferson's favorite words of July 4th, 175 years ago, as "still serving as a beacon paving the way to freedom for oppressed nations and people" and as foundation on which the United States rests its hopes.

A147.   11 July 1952: 5. July the fourth activities, guests, and out-of-towners occupy this column.

A148.   25 July 1952: 5. Local news includes the Fifth Annual Elk's Day celebration at which the Miss Sepia contest of 1952 presented a fashion show "parading professional Philadelphia models."

A149.   8 Aug. 1952: 5. Mrs. Dorothy Cannon DuVaul, a Bridgeville native, is recognized for her musical talents. The sister of Harry "Beavas" Douglas, leader of the internationally known Deep River Boys, Mrs. DuVaul teaches piano in Indianapolis, fills television and radio engagements, and is the accompanist for a dancing school. Her music is "like listening to Hazel Scott and Count Basie combined."

A150.   29 Aug. 1952: 5. Preceding the local news, Shockley gives an update on Harry "Beavas" Douglas and his singing quartet, the Deep River Boys, who are "wowing" the theatergoers at Trivoli in Stockholm, Sweden.

A151.   5 Sept. 1952: 6. Local Labor Day activities are reflected upon.

A152.   12 Sept. 1952: 5. September 17th has been designated as Citizenship Day in commemoration of the formation and signing of the Constitution of the U.S. on September 17, 1787. With the arrival of that day, Shockley advises, "It would be wise for every citizen to reevaluate his contribution as an American to society, taking advantage of whether or not he has fulfilled his capacities as a good, loyal, and responsible citizen...."

A153.   19 Sept. 1952: 5. Marian Anderson was recently awarded Sweden's distinguished but seldom bestowed "Literus et Artibus" decoration which includes a gold medal. King Gustav Adolf in Stockholm presented the award. Shockley notes that Marian Anderson "is one of the finest contralto voices in the country [and] began her singing career in the church in Philadelphia."

A154.   26 Sept. 1952: 6. Marciano defeats Joe Walcott. Shockley writes, Marciano "can be acclaimed as the man who started a new boxing regime by flooring two old champs, Joe Louis and the famed Satchel Paige of boxing, Jersey Joe Walcott." With the flooring of Walcott, one should consider "his struggle for the championship, his numerous detours on his pugilistic journey in the guises of close decisions, and the heart that Walcott possesses." It was his fighting heart that has kept him going.

A155.   3 Oct. 1952: 6. The all-black Gershwin folk opera "Porgy and Bess" receives loud acclaim on its European tour. Two of its operatic selections are "Summer Time" and "I Got Plenty O' Nuttin." This is the "first truly American opera."

A156.   10 Oct 1952: 2. Mention is made of the defeat of the Brooklyn Bums in the World Series against the Yanks. Shockley reminds fans that with the excellent efforts of Joe Black, Jackie Robinson, and Roy Campanella, the Dodgers' fans may have their day of victory next year.

A157.   17 Oct. 1952: 2. The local news includes the announcement of a new slate of officers for the William Paskins American Legion Post 24, a local pre-dawn breakfast party, a dinner party, and a Jason High School football game.

A158.   24 Oct. 1952: 8. Schools and various civic organizations celebrate the seventh anniversary of the United Nations this week; by doing so, writes Shockley, they "are celebrating the foresightedness of the Allied Powers during World War II when these nations discovered that the only way to attempt to preserve that heritage for which they were fighting was by being united."

A159.   31 Oct. 1952: 4. Shockley urges voters to cast their ballots on election day, November 14th, to help shape the country's progress for the next four years. She refers to Elmo Roper, who stated in his Sunday NBC broadcast on June 22nd, "that...the Negro vote can swing the election either way, but that 69 percent of the Negroes have not voted at all in the last four years." Shockley also mentions _Jet_'s claim that "The

Negro in Delaware will be one of the decisive factors
in this...race."

A160.   14 Nov. 1952: 5. Shockley announces the celebration
of Book Week at the local Phillis Wheatley School
where various projects and activities are conducted.
She briefly comments on Homecoming at Delaware State
College; the College's football team, the Delaware
Hornets, was trounced by Howard University, 25-0.

A161.   21 Nov. 1952: 6. In recognition of Book Week, the
Phillis Wheatley School conducts various activities
to emphasize the value of books. Other news focuses
on travel, guests, a banquet, and the fact that
Delaware State College and Jason High School football
teams lost their homecoming games.

A162.   28 Nov. 1952: 6. Thanks are given during the Thanksgiving season for "an increasing fruitful democracy
that is developing in this nation of many people."

A163.   5 Dec. 1952: 4. Shockley reflects on friends and relatives who gathered for the Thankgiving holidays.

A164.   12 Dec. 1952: 6. All are asked to aid in the important
forty-sixth annual Christmas seal sale drive. Purchase
of seals will go toward helping to prevent and control
the spread of tuberculosis. According to the Delaware
Anti-Tuberculosis Society, the colored tuberculosis
rate in Delaware is six times higher than that of
the white race.

A165.   26 Dec. 1952: 4. The yuletide season brings traditional
Christmas caroling, parties, and programs. These and
other local functions are mentioned.

1953

A166.   2 Jan. 1953: 8. The new year begins with an announcement of parties given New Year's eve by the local
black society set and with names of out-of-town
visitors.

A167.   9 Jan. 1953: 6. Shockley notes that we can view with
pride such happenings as "the discontinuing of segregated elementary schools in [various states], the
Medical Association admitting colored professional
members for the first time, a Negro candidate being
elected to the Augusta School Board in Georgia, and
the historic announcement from Tuskegee Institute
that there were no lynchings in this country in 1952
for the first time in 70 years." For 1953, Shockley
suggests that we "optimistically watch the young year
grow and see if it will mature more fully than its
predecessor." Other news looks at out-of-town guests,
dinners, and a testimonial reception.

A168. 16 Jan. 1953: 3. An appeal is made for annual donations
to the March of Dimes drive. Begun in 1938 by the
late President Franklin D. Roosevelt, the March of
Dimes finances medical research, treatment and care
of Infantile Paralysis patients, and an educational
program for doctors and nurses.

A169. 23 Jan. 1953: 6. Shockley bids farewell to Harry S.
Truman as president and wishes that he may continue
to fight for "the great American heritage of democracy." Local news follows.

A170. 6 Feb. 1953: 5. Shockley uses the definitions of
"brotherhood" of three local community leaders to
introduce the celebration of Brotherhood Week. The
definitions are those of Elizabeth C. Dix, English
teacher at Jason High School; Reverend C. H. Kiah,
Pastor of Mt. Calvary Methodist Church; and W. Shockley, teacher and Commander of the American Legion
Post 24.

A171. 13 Feb. 1953: 6. This issue observes Negro History
Week by noting the contributions of such persons as
Dr. Jane Wright, Dr. Ralph Bunche, and Edith Sampson,
"who have not just given their talents as a 'particular' race of people or as a 'particular' addition
to the glory of one special group of people, but as
Americans and for the benefit of all." The local
Phillis Wheatley School observes Negro History Week
by giving attention to local talent: Harry Douglas
and his Deep River Boys and Mrs. Dorothy Cannon, all
of whom have made a name for themselves in the music
world.

A172. 20 Feb. 1953: 5. Shockley announces the organizing
of a central Delaware chapter of the NAACP composed
of members from Kent, Sussex, and lower New Castle
counties. She gives the importance of the NAACP and
reminds her readers of its court battles since 1909.
Other comments include the appearance of Harry Douglas
and his Deep River Boys on the Kate Smith television
show and the televised Chuck Davey and the Kid Gavilan
fight.

A173. 27 Feb. 1953: 2. Shockley gives the setting of and
attendance at the second annual dance of the Seaford Frederick Douglass School Faculty Club. Chuck
Smith's orchestra performed at the affair.

A174. 6 Mar. 1953: 5. Two meetings were recently held by
the NAACP regarding racial concerns. One was to discuss
plans to secure community support for the integration
of Delaware public schools in various counties; the
other was to discuss future plans for Delaware State
College with Governor Bogus and the Sussex Alumni
Association. Governor Bogus offered several suggestions
for the school; among them were to make it "an ac-
credited institution, a trade school, a junior college,
or [merge] it with the University of Delaware."

A175.   13 Mar. 1953: 2. A dance sponsored by the American
         Legion William Paskins Post 24 and its auxiliary
         will not only benefit the legion, but also offer the
         community entertainment.

A176.   20 Mar. 1953: 4. Shockley comments that "Jazz is re-
         turning and is here to stay." Whether jazz will have
         another heyday as it did in the 1920's, when Louis
         Armstrong, King Oliver, Eddie Condon, and Benny Goodman
         were playing, is difficult to say. Johnny Sparrow,
         who formerly played with Louis Armstrong and Lionel
         Hampton, will perform with his band at the dance spon-
         sored by the William Paskins American Legion Post
         24 and its auxiliary.

A177.   27 Mar. 1953: 6. Three items are important. First,
         the Central Delaware National Association for the
         Advancement of Colored People has organized in Dover;
         Reverend Dr. Grant Shockley is President. Secondly,
         the Sussex Branch of the NAACP will "lobby for
         the FEPC bill which is due to come up on the floor
         soon,... and efforts will be made to have work done
         on the state owned roads in Negro communities which
         are in dire need of repairing." Third, the 125th
         anniversary of the founding of the first black news-
         paper was celebrated by the National Newspaper Pub-
         lishers Association; annual awards were given honoring
         John B. Russworm, founder and editor of Freedom's
         Journal, the first black newspaper.

A178.   3 Apr. 1953: 4. Shockley makes a tribute to Easter
         as a time when "one can renew his faith in himself
         and realize that the good that can triumph over Easter
         is revealed and revived in the story of Easter and
         its moralistic reawakening of salvation."

A179.   17 Apr. 1953: 4. Local news captures a Laurel Roger
         Gumby American Legion Post Dance, a birth, and Young
         Adult Day at Mt. Calvary Methodist Church.

A180.   24 Apr. 1953: 2. Two important events mentioned are
         the banquet held by the Rising Sun Lodge and the Child
         Welfare Conference of the American Legion and its
         auxiliary.

A181.   1 May 1953: 4. Dr. W. Faulkner, Dean of the Chapel
         of Fisk University, and Dr. Charles S. Johnson, Presi-
         dent of Fisk, launched the United Negro College Fund
         drive in Delaware. In a WDEL radio interview, Dr.
         Faulkner pointed out that thirty-one "Negro institu-
         tions of higher learning would rather accept private
         donations than state or federal grants because of
         their firm belief in academic freedom." To these
         colleges, Shockley learned later from a UNCF letter
         that she received, the 1952 UNCF drive brought nearly
         a million dollars in gifts and grants.

A182.   8 May 1953: 6. Shockley brings to the community's
         attention the notice Africa has received in <u>Life</u>
         magazine. Africa is recognized as a continent of change
         in which "civilization...is gradually penetrating
         the land. Africa, too, is entering her plea for man
         to treat man as man in order that human dignity may
         survive."

A183.   22 May 1953: 4. Shockley comments on a recent <u>Time</u>
         magazine issue devoted to blacks' progress. She agrees
         that the "greatest fight of the Negro in the past
         decade has been for simple decent treatment in everyday
         life." She quotes Gunnar Myrdal as saying, "...if
         America in actual practice could show the world that
         the Negro became finally integrated into modern democ-
         racy, all mankind would be given faith again."

A184.   29 May 1953: 2. In 1943, Dr. F.D. Patterson, President
         of Tuskegee Institute, Tuskegee, Alabama, conceived
         of the idea for private black colleges to join in
         a united appeal for financial help. By 1944, the United
         Negro College Fund started as a means of calling
         nationwide attention to these schools and their needs.
         Shockley appeals to all to contribute to the United
         Negro College Fund drive.

A185.   5 June 1953: 3. In 1953, Paul Williams, noted Los
         Angeles architect, was awarded the Spingarn Medal.
         He will be honored with a gold medallion at the forty-
         fourth annual NAACP convention in St. Louis, June
         23-28. The award is given each year to a black who
         has reached the highest achievement in his field.
         Previous winners have been Ralph Bunche, Paul Robeson,
         Percy Julian, and Mary McLeod Bethune.

A186.   12 June 1953: 3. Among announcements of commencement
         exercises and the Boy Scouts Camporee is that of the
         testimonial banquet honoring Mrs. Elizabeth H. Shockley
         of Milford, retiring from the school system after
         more than thirty-five years of teaching. She is the
         mother of W.L. Shockley of Bridgeville; A.H. Shockley
         of Milford, Principal of Laurel's Paul Dunbar School;
         and Mrs. Elizabeth S. Palmer of Milford, teacher at
         Frankford Elementary School. The retiree is Ann Allen
         Shockley's mother-in-law.

A187.   26 June 1953: 2. Shockley pays tribute to Dads on
         Father's Day. She writes this is the day Dad can "sit
         in a favorite chair without a tie, smoke his smelly
         pipe, and even look or listen to a double header base-
         ball game minus interruptions from Mom and Junior."

A188.   3 July 1953: 7. Shockley believes that of all the
         words for liberty written by men, the most inspiring
         are those comprising the Declaration of Independence.
         This document, writes Shockley, "did much to stir
         the hearts of the early colonists, and today, the
         words embodied in the Declaration have been molded

into the minds of freethinking people all over the world."

A189.   10 July 1953: 3. Brought to Shockley's attention was an article appearing in <u>Evening Journal</u> [Wilmington, DE] on May 25th concerning Mrs. Emma Cannon, believed to be the oldest living person in Delaware. Friends of Mrs. Cannon want it mentioned that she is well-known in Bridgeville and in Laurel, where she has lived for some time. Mrs. Cannon is estimated to be 109 or 111 years old. She resides at the Layton Home for aged persons.

A190.   24 July 1953: 3. Jack Johnson, as a boxing great, heads the news with Shockley referring to an article on Johnson's career and life in <u>Our Sport</u> magazine. Other news includes the weather, vacations, and entertainment.

A191.   31 July 1953: 2. A dog lover, Shockley facetiously dedicates this week's column to what is "occurring in the local social world of dogs." A newcomer in town is Garbage Can Pete, visiting along with his master and mistress, Mr. and Mrs. Leon DuVaul of Indiana. He is the guest of Mrs. Carrie Cannon, grandmother of Mrs. DuVaul. Shockley tells how the mutt acquired his name and holds a conversation with him by "watching his tail, ears, and eyes."

A192.   7 Aug. 1953: 4. This week's news offers two eating tips for entertaining women with guests.

A193.   21 Aug. 1953: 5. Shockley announces the appointments of Philip Sadler of Wilmington as racial consultant for the Federal Housing Program and Mrs. Mary Cannon, President of the local William Paskins American Legion Auxiliary Post 24, to fourth Vice President of the state auxiliary.

A194.   28 Aug. 1953: 4. The famed Harlem Globetrotters performed before a crowd of four thousand in Wilmington last week. A local wedding and traveling conclude the news.

A195.   4 Sept. 1953: 8. Shockley refers to the August 31st issue of <u>Time</u> magazine and the watchful eye that magazine is keeping on segregated schools. She observes that the aftermath of the breakdown of racial barriers was not as inflammatory as many predicted.

A196.   18 Sept. 1953: 8. Harry Douglas and his Deep River Boys play before capacity crowds in Europe. The latest news is that Savanah Churchill is to join the group. Labor Day guests and vacationers head local news.

A197.   25 Sept. 1953: 4. All persons are urged to cooperate in the mobile X-ray program sponsored by the state to improve the community's health.

A198.   23 Oct. 1953: 4. Billie Holiday's television appearance
         on Comeback heads the news. Shockley mentions an aura
         of sadness and age permeating Holiday as she told
         her life's story. Holiday's appearance comes after
         her fall as a drug addict and signals her attempt
         to rise again. Shockley muses that Holiday "sang in
         her old way, once described by someone as a woman
         who sings like her shoes are too tight." Count Basie
         provided the musical background for the show.

A199.   30 Oct. 1953: 3. Local schools and organizations
         observe United Nations Week with celebrations. Shockley
         cites "the celebration of the Eighth Anniversary of
         the signing of the UN Charter as another notch upon
         the milestone of human relations." She views the
         United Nations as having "promoted better economic,
         social, and cultural understanding between nations
         along with its gigantic task of maintaining peace."
         "Not since the Crusades," concludes Shockley, "have
         so many people of such various countries bonded to-
         gether for the purpose of keeping the principle of
         Christian idealism alive."

A200.   6 Nov. 1953: 4. As she announces the eightieth birthday
         of blind W.C. Handy and his thirty-fifth year as a
         Broadway music publisher, Shockley remembers his visit
         to Fisk University when she was a student there. She
         reflects that Handy played his famed "St. Louis Blues"
         without embellishment, without accompaniment, and
         a little off-beat for his wind wasn't as strong as
         it once was."

A201.   20 Nov. 1953: 5. Mt. Calvary Methodist Church cele-
         brated its eighty-second anniversary last Sunday.
         Shockley notes the history of the church, its finan-
         cial status and its important activities.

A202.   27 Nov. 1953: 5. In observance of Thanksgiving,
         Shockley affirms that "Thanksgiving should commemorate
         the blessings of free living, free thought, and the
         tremendous efforts put forth now and before by all
         to maintain these fundamentals which make up a free
         nation."

A203.   4 Dec. 1953: 7. Announcements are made of the B'nai
         B'rith Anti-Defamation League presenting President
         Eisenhower with a civil liberties award and of Roy
         Campanella's election as baseball's most valuable
         player.

A204.   18 Dec. 1953: 5. James Evans has been elected as
         Commander of the William Paskins American Legion Post
         24. He assumes the duties of past Commanders Louis
         Ricketts and W. L. Shockley, Sr. He is a World War
         II veteran, a Delaware State College graduate, and
         principal at Richard Allen Elementary School in
         Georgetown.

A205.   25 Dec. 1953: 8. Shockley extends Christmas cheer
         to all; it is the most "beautiful time of the year."

1954

A206.   1 Jan. 1954: 8. Notices are given of yuletide affairs.

A207.   8 Jan. 1954: 4. Shockley records the progress that
        blacks made in race relations in 1953, particularly
        with the breakdown of segregation in colleges, armed
        forces, public housing, and government positions.
        The biggest step toward testing full integration
        will come, she says, "when the Supreme Court hands
        down its decision on segregated schools."

A208.   15 Jan. 1954: 4. This column highlights a 230 pound,
        9 point buck shot by a one-eyed local hunter, James
        "Sparky" Rick. The entire episode is incredible to
        Shockley, whose closest distance to killing a duck
        is her "half-hearted attempt to knock down one of
        the slowly moving ducks found on a carnival shooting
        range." Sparky attributes his good marksmanship to
        his one eye. Delaware's largest deer killed this
        hunting season was felled on January 1st.

A209.   22 Jan. 1954: 5. Harry "Beavas" Douglas and his group,
        whom Shockley refers to as "the singing 'Globe Trot-
        ters,'" appeared on Red Buttons television show.
        Mention is made also of Donald Waters, another Bridge-
        ville man who is beginning to reach for "a star studded
        musical career"; he formed his own combo, while serving
        at Fairchild Base in Spokane, Washington.

A210.   12 Feb. 1954: 4. Local citizens define "brotherhood"
        during Brotherhood Week. Other local news follows.

A211.   19 Feb. 1954: 4. Local social events head the news:
        a baby shower, the Gun and Rod Club dance, and a sur-
        prised birthday party.

A212.   5 Mar. 1954: 4. Local news includes birthday parties,
        military men home on leave, the success of men's day
        at Mt. Calvary Methodist Church, the meeting of the
        American Legion Post 24 Auxiliary, and the annual
        Debutante's Ball, given by the Wilmington Zeta Omega
        Chapter of the Alpha Kappa Alpha Sorority.

A213.   12 Mar. 1954: 5. The Third Annual Seaford Faculty
        Dance headlines the news. Other social events include
        luncheons, cocktails, and fashion shows.

A214.   19 Mar. 1954: 5. The column zeroes in March 15th
        issue of _Life_ magazine, which contains an article
        on the recent shooting of five congressmen by Puerto
        Rican nationalist Pedro Campos. _Life's_ statement that
        "Pedro Campos harbored a seed of hatred for America
        sprouting from the roots of his being treated like
        a Negro while serving as a soldier during World War
        I" leads Shockley to editorialize. She uses the Campos

situation as a springboard to state that blacks have "never previously resorted to such unmitigated action... We can be proud of the levelheadedness of our leaders and ourselves in the battle for the rights of first class citizens. We know the worth of courts...."

A215.   26 Mar. 1954: 8. Fashion shows, exhibits, and traveling dominate the news. This is Shockley's last column, but there is no mention that "Ebony Topics" will be discontinued.

NEWSPAPER FEATURE STORIES

A216.   "Florida Teacher Is Home for Vacation." Louisville
        Defender 7 July 1945: N. pag.

        For her first feature story, Shockley interviewed
        Mary Carolyn Cox (sometimes called "Cally"), Louisville
        native and Fisk University graduate on vacation from
        her teaching duties at Howard Academy in Ocala,
        Florida. Shockley captures the slow, soft-spoken drawl
        of this young woman who recounts the beauty and seren-
        ity of the Florida town that was once an Indian settle-
        ment. Chosen as feature story subject because of her
        social prominence, Miss Cox nostalgically muses that
        she has missed old friends in Louisville and the city's
        social life. The story is presented in simple, matter-
        of-fact language.

A217.   "Bored Housewives." Louisville Defender July 1945:
        N. pag.

        The author is unsympathetic to the bored housewives
        whose numbers will increase in the postwar period,
        as factory jobs for women phase out when men return
        from war. Shockley believes that housewives who talk
        on the telephone, play bridge, and join clubs to escape
        boredom are not making "wise usage of leisure time."
        Referring to them as "Gunpowder" women, Shockley claims
        that they will explode if more productive use is not
        made of their time.

A218.   "Civil Air Patrol Is in Summer Encampment." Louisville
        Defender July 1945: N. pag.

        Shockley reports that on July 16, 1945, "the summer
        encampment of Kentucky's Civil Air Patrol cadets,
        conducted with the assistance of the Army Air Forces,
        began at Bowman Field, Louisville, and will continue
        until July 29." The cadets provide their own trans-
        portation to and from Bowman Field, furnish their
        uniforms, and pay for their food. Bowman Field provides
        housing, classrooms, and recreational facilities.
        The American Air Force provides training, textbooks,
        and field and technical manuals. There are fifty-five
        cadets, eighteen of which are blacks, ranging in ages
        from fifteen to seventeen. The leader of Squadron
        Six, eighteen-year-old First Sergeant John W. Hagan,
        has thirty cadets under his command.

A219.   "Bowman Field Aids Training of Youth Air Aspirants."
        Louisville Defender July 1945: N. pag.

        This is a follow-up on the CAP cadets at Bowman Field.
        The cadets have received instructions in first aid,
        air craft instruments, ground safety, and sanitation.
        Participating fully in military life, the cadets have
        had standing inspections.

A220. "A Day with the Nurses at Nichols." Louisville Defender
       July 1945: N. pag.

       To write this story, Shockley spent the day at Nichols
       General Hospital. She reports on the routine involved
       in a regular working day of army nurses and describes
       their living quarters.

A221. "Junior Miss a Joy in American Life." Louisville
       Defender July 1945: N. pag.

       This story explores the world of Junior Miss, better
       known as the "bobby sox." Readers are apprised of
       what she eats, what music she listens to, what her
       ploys are for escaping dishwashing, and what she does
       on first dates. She "makes life worth living for mother
       and death a peaceful thought to father."

A222. "Men and Women Are People, People Are Strange Things."
       Louisville Defender July 1945: N. pag.

       This story concerns the contradictions displayed by
       young matrons who want to be admired by the opposite
       sex, but become annoyed when men publicly display
       their affections for them. It was written in response
       to an "SOS signal" sent by three Seattle women to
       the "Mules and Men Department" of the Chicago Herald
       American asking it to organize an association for
       the improvement of married men's conduct. Shockley
       comments that when men fail to show their appreciation
       of women, "milady thinks she's losing what she thought
       she once had; and when the old or young gay blade
       whistles, milady says he's fresh." The humorous con-
       clusion is : "People are funny, aren't we?" A cartoon
       drawn by the staff cartoonist accompanies this story.

A223. "Officers' Lounge Formally Opened." Louisville
       Defender July 1945: N. pag.

       Shockley announces the opening of the Beecher Terrace
       Officers' Lounge, July 7th, at the Parish House of
       the Church of Our Merciful Savior. The lounge is for
       the use of officers stationed in the Louisville area
       and for the nurses at Nichols General Hospital.

A224. "Our Men." Louisville Defender July 1945: N. pag.

       An inked notation in Shockley's scrapbook indicates
       that this story "is a 'pickup' I wrote from the
       Chicago Herald American." The contents refer to a
       very conservative department store in Chicago that
       has "the most elegant assortment of all the stuff
       [for men] that used to be for women only." Shockley
       tells us that a shortage of materials has men wearing
       ladies' panties, and she reminds wives to watch their
       cosmetics and lingerie before they "will have a short-
       age of everything."

A225. "Police Rule 'No Go' for Bare Midriffs." Louisville
       Defender July 1945: N. pag.

       This is Shockley's first front page story. It reminds
       all women that the Louisville Police Department does
       not allow women to walk in public with shorts on and
       midriffs exposed. Women "may end up in the calaboose
       for disorderly conduct for the lowering of the morals
       of the community and indecent exposure of the body."
       She reports that while Chicago and Texas "believe
       in the body beautiful," a judge in New York recently
       fined a twenty-three year old two dollars "because
       she had her midriff out for an airing."

A226. "Summer Hair Style." Louisville Defender July 1945:
       N. pag.

       Information for this story was gathered from a hair-
       dresser who indicated that women prefer the pompadour
       roll or upsweep hairstyle in the summer and that the
       young set likes brush curls, pompadours, and pageboys.
       As for hair processing, college students like the
       marcel. This is an important piece for its information
       on black hairstyles in the 1940's.

A227. "With 'Joe College' Missing, Campus Life Is Not the
       Same." Louisville Defender July 1945: N. pag.

       Shockley notes in her scrapbook that this feature
       had to be censored by her editor because of "some
       facts I had in it." She refused a by-line because
       of her comments. The story concerns how college women
       feel about filling campus positions, traditionally
       held by men who are now away at war. The women seem
       not to mind assuming such positions as president of
       Student Union Government or editors of college papers,
       but they consider the male shortage deplorable. Of
       the few men left, one co-ed remarks, "Whatta shortage!
       Girls just grab!" This insightful story gives a sense
       of how black co-eds from various American colleges
       and universities in the 1940's felt about campus life.

A228. "Youngsters Enjoy Long Outing among Hills at Camp
       Ski-Hi." Louisville Defender July 1945: N. pag.

       This story features a four-week camping trip at Camp
       Ski-Hi, located several miles from Louisville. Boys
       on the trip enjoy recreational activities best. They
       study nature, swim, play ball, hike, and make handi-
       crafts.

A229. "This Is Nashville." Give Me a Name 8 Nov. 1947: 1+.

       A moving story on race mixing in segregated Nashville
       in the 1940's, it captures the interdependence of
       Anna Pollenard (a black woman) and Ninny Hipton
       (a white woman), who live next door to each other
       on Fisk Street, a crooked, unpaved corridor lined

with two-room shacks and outhouses. While Ninny Hipton
picks cotton in Arkansas, Anna Pollenard keeps her
step-children for "ten or twelve dollars at irregular
intervals." Hinton and Pollenard "pass butter, sugar,
and milk over the termite eaten fence to each other,"
their borrowing indicating hard times for both black
and white. During the interview, Anna Pollenard and
her other white neighbor relate to Shockley that "there
is no hope in the south for racial equality." Both
look down on well-to-do whites and blacks, whom they
agree do nothing for poor people. The irony of this
story is that poor blacks and whites in "The Bottom,"
as this section of Nashville was called, had more
in common than many realized the two races had. To
make this point, Shockley includes stark realism,
faithfulness to details, and an element of surprise,
all of which characterize her fiction.

A230.   "Just Thinking." Give Me a Name 8 Nov. 1947: 3+.
Shockley's early feminism shines in this piece about
American women who have remained silent about recent
political, religious, or social change, but have staged
protests against male designers' dropping the hemlines
of women's dresses. She favors more political and
social action on the part of American women who greatly
outnumber men and are "buried in kitchens...." She
feels that women have been too "content to be pampered
by man so that he can think he is lord and master
while he is merely being used as a tool for [the
attainment of] a home, car, clothes, and meal ticket."
When women do act, man has no chance to win -- "he
will concede merely to shut them up." Shockley concludes that women are not as dead as their inertia
suggests and "when provoked, are perfectly capable
of swift and violent action."

LETTERS

A231. "Medievalism and This Atomic Age." Fisk University
       Herald 40 (Oct. 1946): 2-3.

       Shockley questions Fisk University's rigid dress code
       for women that prevents them from wearing to classes
       "slacks, jeans, and pedal pushers." It is her opinion
       that Fiskites should be recognized for their "ideas,
       behavior, and intelligence," and not for what is worn.
       "If this is a community of one big happy family,"
       she writes, "it should be an informal one and not
       a conglomeration of people ruled over by a stiff,
       formal, and outdated set of notions."

A232. "He Has Seen a Light Shining." Evening Journal
       [Wilmington, DE] 4 Aug. 1964: 30.

       Shockley reflects on the historical oppression of
       American blacks and comments on recent black distur-
       bances in Wilmington: "I was glad this bitterness
       was made known but not in this way or at this time."
       She condones neither violence nor hatred toward man,
       but "can understand this grim bitterness even though
       I have never experienced many of the intolerable
       conditions borne by thousands of my people." Only
       when racial issues are dealt with by "responsible
       and knowledgeable people of both races" will the health
       of our country improve.

A233. "A Dream Shattered." Evening Journal [Wilmington, DE]
       14 June 1968: 24.

       Saddened by the deaths of President John F. Kennedy,
       Reverend Martin Luther King, and Senator Robert F.
       Kennedy, Shockley writes, "These beautiful men...
       will live on in the ideas perpetuated, the dreams
       envisioned, and...the beautiful lives left behind."

A234. Focus [Boston, MA] Nov. 1975: 2.

       Shockley reacts to J. S.'s essay "Different Ways of
       Being Different," published in the September 1975
       issue of Focus. She disagrees with the use of Ralph
       Ellison's novel to develop the thesis "there are simi-
       larities between gays and other minority groups in
       their recognition and affirmation of self." Such an
       approach, answers Shockley, "showed considerable
       naiveness." Shockley contends that discrimination
       against blacks growing up in a racist society is much
       greater than that against gays growing up in a hetero-
       sexual society. The letter is important in pointing
       up a false analogy.

A235. Black Scholar 9 (July-Aug. 1978): 54.

       This letter is written in response to Audre Lorde's

article "Scratching the Surface: Some Notes on Barriers to Women and Loving," published in <u>Black Scholar</u>, April 1978. In her one-sentence letter, Shockley says simply, "I congratulate you on publishing Audre Lorde's sensitive article."

ESSAYS

A236. "Does the Negro College Library Need a Special Negro
       Collection?" Library Journal 86 (1 June 1961): 2049-
       50.

       This essay documents the findings of a questionnaire
       Maryland State College Library sent to other black
       college libraries to determine the need for a special
       black collection on their campuses. The responses
       varied and were dependent on such factors as individual
       budgets, gifts, and student attitudes. Shockley pro-
       fessionally and correctly concludes that if a black
       college is unable to have an inclusive collection,
       then it should have black collections in special aca-
       demic areas. Accompanying this essay are a photograph
       of the Negro Collection at Maryland State College
       (now University of Maryland Eastern Shore) and
       Shockley's photograph.

A237. "Reading Encouragement in the Maryland State College
       Library." Maryland Libraries 28 (Spring 1962): 13+.

       This article discusses the ploys used by the library
       staff at Maryland State College to increase student
       use of the library. Among the important enticements
       mentioned are creating an atmosphere of comfort and
       informality, making books available that have been
       banned through the years for immorality, operating
       an open stack system, and initiating book discussions.
       That this essay had to be written suggests that
       laziness and disinterest breed laziness and disinterest
       and that Shockley dislikes both.

A238. "Student Assistants in a Small College Library."
       Maryland Libraries 30 (Winter 1964): 16-17.

       The advantages and disadvantages of student assistants
       working in the library are the issues here. Shockley
       concludes that a student's grade-point average does
       not necessarily indicate whether a student will make
       a good assistant and that the proper training,
       guidance, and interest are invaluable assets that
       each student assistant must have. Shockley does
       not mention the stations that student assistants should
       be assigned to in the library, and this omission
       appears to be a weakness in this essay. The very nature
       of the reference section requires a trained librarian
       to be in attendance at all times; and student assis-
       tants, regardless of their training, would not, to
       my thinking, have the best service to offer clients.

A239. "The Role of Book Bulletins in a Small College
       Library." Maryland Libraries 31 (Spring 1965): 7-9.

       Inspired by poor faculty use of the library, this
       article champions the employment of book bulletins

on a small college campus to publicize library holdings. The appearance of the bulletin is important,
but Shockley maintains that a listing of the library's
new editions can be done on mimeographed paper. This
essay is one of several in which Shockley intended
to inspire a better attitude toward the library.

A240. "The Negro Woman in Retrospect: Blueprint for the
Future." Negro History Bulletin 29 (Dec. 1965): 55+.

After assessing the humble circumstances from which
the black woman has emerged, Shockley acknowledges
the professions in which black women have made great
strides and predicts the black woman's move toward
full equality. Because this essay is an overview,
it does not have the substance that her more focused
pieces have. Yet it is characterized by accurate docu-
mentation, appropriate statistics, and unbiased re-
portage.

A241. "Negro Librarians in Predominantly Negro Colleges."
College and Research Libraries 28 (Nov. 1967): 423-
26.

This informative article is the result of a survey
Shockley conducted to obtain the background and
attitudes of black librarians toward librarianship.
The study reveals blacks are a minority in the field
of librarianship owing to a history of poor training
opportunities and unjust employment practices. The
general attitude of the group surveyed is that black
librarians do not wish to be considered as "a different
breed," but as librarians.

A242. "The Reading Habits of Upward Bound Students at Maryland State College." Maryland Libraries 35 (Fall 1968):
17-18.

To determine the reading backgrounds of Upward Bound
Students at Maryland State College in Princess Anne
County, the library staff at the college prepared
a questionnaire for those students enrolled in the
June 1968 program. The responses to the questionnaire
revealed that these students did have some form of
home library, but did not have enough books, and that
students generally preferred to read books on the
black experience. Shockley concludes that the reading
skills of these Upward Bound Students can be enhanced
considerably if they are given selected books "to
explore the wide range of exciting reading vistas."
This conclusion is not new, as is indicated in Shockley's example of Claude Brown, a black author who
was inspired to read while serving time in Warwick
Reformatory in New York. The essay's significance
is its reemphasizing an old and tested method that
has produced positive results.

A243.   "Two Books with Soul: For Defiant Ones." English
         Journal 58 (Mar. 1969): 396-98. Rpt. in Contemporary
         Literary Criticism. Ed. Jean C. Stine and G. Marowski.
         Detroit: Gale, 1984. 30: 38.

         Shockley points up comparisons between two ethnically
         different biographies, Claude Brown's Manchild in
         a Promised Land (Macmillan, 1967) and Piri Thomas'
         Down These Mean Streets (Knopf, 1967). Both Claude
         Brown and Piri Thomas came from impoverished back-
         grounds and took to the streets out of desperation.
         Although Brown is a black from Harlem and Thomas is
         a Puerto Rican from Spanish Harlem, both encountered
         a similar racism because of skin color, and both agreed
         that the Muslim Movement of the 1960's brought meaning
         and purpose to their lives. The most striking parallel
         that Shockley gleans from these two works is that
         both men managed to survive the sordidness of their
         lives. A comparison of books across ethnic lines is
         seldom attempted by black American women critics,
         and, for this reason, Shockley's essay is important.

A244.   "Tell It Like It Is: New Criteria for Children's Books
         in Black and White." Southeastern Librarian 20 (Spring
         1970): 30-33.

         Shockley carefully analyzes the negative effects of
         the Sambo image on the developing minds of white child-
         ren since the presentation of this image in Helen
         Bannerman's Little Black Sambo in 1900. She then gives
         pertinent criteria for children's books about blacks,
         among which are realism and black English. She cites
         John Steptoe's Stevie and Jan Wagner's J.T. as good
         examples of children's books about blacks and concludes
         that black librarians should demand from publishers
         books relevant to the black experience.

A245.   "A Soul Cry for Reading." in The Black Librarian in
         America. Ed. E.J. Josey. Metuchen: Scarecrow P, 1970.
         225-33.

         In this semi-autobiographical essay, Shockley cites
         the joy reading has brought her and the need for black
         librarians, black teachers, and black students to
         read more. With a convincing message, an urgent tone,
         and earnest sincerity, she tells blacks that through
         reading they "share the real wealth, the heritage
         of mankind." She focuses most of the essay on her
         Eastern Shore experiences at Delaware State College
         and Maryland State College (now University of Mary-
         land Eastern Shore) and allows the reader a rare
         glimpse into her life as an underpaid, overworked
         librarian or "general factotum," as she titles herself.

A246.   "Establishing Black Collections for Black Studies."
         College Library Notes 11 (Spring 1971): 1-4.

         To librarians whose academic libraries do not have
         adequate black collections necessary to meet the read-

ing demands of developing Black Studies Programs, Shockley addresses this essay. Her basic accurate assumption is that "Many of these black collections are being staffed by librarians who know nothing about black history, black books or black people." Her words of warning, therefore, are in order. She cautions librarians against buying exorbitantly priced reprints by unethical publishers and suggests a good reprint series, The American Negro: His History and Literature, published by Arno Press and New York Times. She admonishes librarians for ordering poorly written books published by commercial publishers and recommends good books published by reputable publishing houses and university presses. She then lists twelve criteria for judging books to be included in a standard black collection and offers eleven bibliographies and guides to aid in the selection of books. The essay concludes with the librarians' responsibility to promote books after acquiring them and to pursue courses in Black Studies to broaden their knowledge in the area. If followed, Shockley's suggestions can build enviable, scholarly resources in black studies.

A247.   "Pauline Elizabeth Hopkins: A Biographical Excursion into Obscurity." Phylon 33 (Spring 1972): 22-26.

More than fifteen years have passed since this essay was published, yet it remains the fullest biographical sketch recorded of Pauline Elizabeth Hopkins, an early black woman writer from Portland, Maine. It scans Hopkins' life from her uncertainly dated birth (1859?) to her tragic death by fire in Cambridge, Massachusetts, August 13, 1930. Pauline Hopkins was first introduced to the public as a writer at fifteen years old, when she won for her essay "The Evils of Intemperance and Their Remedy" ten dollars in gold offered by Willaim Wells Brown, representing the Congregational Publishing Society of Boston. She performed with the Hopkins' Colored Troubadours, a family group, for which she wrote the drama Slaves' Escape: or the Underground Railroad (1879). Another play she wrote, but did not produce, is One Scene from the Drama of Early Days. Shockley does not enter a date for this play.

Pauline Hopkins' career as a fiction writer began in her forties. She is best known for her novel Contending Forces, some copies of which the publisher circulated free of charge. She also published two others, Winona: A Tale of Negro Life in the South and Southwest in the 1840's and Of One Blood or the Hidden Self, both serialized in Colored American, of which she became literary editor. She wrote six short stories, three of which Shockley brings to our attention: "Talma Gordon," "George Washington: A Christmas Story," and "Bro'r Abr'm Jimson's Wedding, A Christmas Story." Despite Hopkins' considerable literary output for a black woman during the last century, no local obituaries appeared in the New

England town where she spent most of her life. This
essay is a valuable research tool; it discloses the
difficulty a nineteenth century Northern black woman
had in establishing herself as a writer and as a
person.

A248.   "Black Book Reviewing: A Case for Library Action."
College and Research Libraries 35 (Jan. 1974): 16-
20. Rpt. in Library Lit. 5--The Best of 1974. Ed.
Bill Katz and Robert Burgess. New York: Scarecrow
P, 1975. 407-14.

Inherent in this essay is Shockley's lament that
standard reference works written by whites "give little
attention to reviewing books by and about blacks,"
and, therefore, librarians are oftentimes handicapped
in choosing and ordering books for the library on
the black experience. She cites reasons why many black
books do not get the attention of the reviewing
channels, lists the qualifications of a book for inclusion in Book Review Digest, names indexes that
do refer to black books and journals, and criticizes
publishers for publishing shoddy books on the black
experience, many with similar and confusing titles.
Most important, Shockley does not relieve black
librarians of their responsibilities in obtaining
for their libraries good books on the black experience.
She offers a set of criteria that librarians should
follow to obtain better books on the black experience
and to understand better indexing and reviewing proce-
dures for these books. For its wise advice, this essay
should be read by all acquisitions librarians.

A249.   "American Anti-Slavery Literature: An Overview-- 1693-
1859." Negro History Bulletin 37 (Apr.-May 1974):
232-35.

Shockley divides anti-slavery literature into three
periods: Colonial Period (1693-1763), Revolutionary
Period (1765-1787), and Ante-Bellum period (1816-1859).
The dates, as well as the subject matter dealt with,
determine these categories. Anti-slavery literature
of the colonial period displays a religious tone and
a brotherhood-of-men theme; it is written mostly by
religion-conscious men such as George Keith, John
Woolman, and Benjamin Rush. Anti-slavery literature
of the revolutionary period shifts to secular content,
focusing on the inalienable rights of man, including
the black man, as espoused by Thomas Paine, David
Cooper, and Jupiter Hammon. The literature of the
Ante-bellum period dramatizes the cruelty and evils
of slavery; its abolitionist newspapers Philanthropist,
Manumission Intelligencer, Liberator, and Emancipator
became organs for the expression of this literature.
It is this body of anti-slavery literature, contends
Shockley, that "was a dominant factor in bringing

to the minds and hearts of people that slavery was
morally wrong and a terrible stigma upon the nation."
Too short to be substantive, this essay, nevertheless,
gives a good overview of anti-slavery literature in
pre-Civil War America.

A250.   Tucker, Veronica, ed. "Black Women Discuss Today's
Problems: Men, Families, Society." Southern Voices
1 (Aug.-Sept. 1974): 16-19.

This essay explores the issues discussed at the first
National Conference on Black Women, held March 7-9,
1974, at the University of Louisville. More than twenty
seminars, panels, and lectures steered attendees to
field questions concerning the relationship between
black men and women. The issues raised were the pre-
requisites to marriage, the role of the black woman
in a relationship with an egotistical man, and the
lack of communal support for the black lesbian. There
was disagreement on many issues, but members of the
conference generally agreed "that the black woman
has a prominent role in society, and that she is the
one to shape, evaluate, and mold this function by
refuting myth-distorted images." The importance of
this essay is that it records issues and responses
pertinent to black life at a conference coordinated
by a black man who calls himself a "new leftist black
historian."

A251.   "The New Black Feminists." Northwest Journal of Africa
and Black America Studies 2 (Winter 1974): 1-5.

Shockley identifies the National Black Feminist Organization, founded in New York City in 1973, and records
its definition of feminism as "...the belief of the
political, economic and social equality of the sexes."
While this definition does not differ significantly
from that of the Women's Liberation Movement, the
black feminists are concerned about black women's
problems in racist, sexist America, and they have
a platform of sixteen priority items. Shockley contends
that there is no attempt on the part of black feminists
to undercut the Women's Liberation Movement, but rather
to give it credibility. She attacks the stereotyped
misconceptions of the term "feminists" and maintains
that black feminists are molding a new image and promoting the best in womanhood.

A252.   "Joseph S. Cotter, Sr., Biographical Sketch of a Black
Louisville Bard." CLA Journal 18 (Mar. 1975): 327-
40.

Considerable research went into the construction of
this biographical sketch of Joseph S. Cotter, Sr.,
black poet, playwright, songwriter, and educator,
who lived from 1861 until 1949. Kentucky newspapers,
the Black Oral History Collection at Fisk University,
the collection of Cotter's papers housed at the Louis-

ville Free Public library (Western Branch), and
Cotter's voluminous writings were some of the sources
used. From these documents, Shockley sketches an edu-
cated and talented humanitarian whose writings have
not received the attention they deserve. An interesting
feature of this essay is Cotter's personal eccentri-
cities.

A253.   "A Necessary Union: Black Publishers and Librarians."
Black World 26 (Mar. 1975): 38-44.

Shockley correctly maintains that libraries are the
largest consumers of books and that there should be
a more equitable relationship between book publishers
and librarians. This argument is used as a springboard
to a more specific argument-- "Black publishers need
to work more closely with librarians." Since books
published by black publishers are not usually reviewed
in traditional channels and since there is sometimes
a time lag of two years between the publication of
a book by a black publisher and its review in a black
journal, Shockley suggests that black publishers send
review copies and catalogs to libraries. Other helpful
suggestions are black publishers should advertise
their books in professional library publications,
utilize booths at professional meetings attended by
librarians, and ask librarians to review books. These
and other suggestions make this an insightful essay
on how librarians and black book publishers can
establish a better relationship and increase sales
of black books.

A254.   "The Best Seller List and Black Authors." In Handbook
of Black Librarianship 153-54.

This essay mentions several works by black authors
on the best seller list. It begins with Richard
Wright's autobiography Black Boy (1945) and ends with
Maya Angelou's I Know Why the Caged Bird Sings (1970).
(Since the publication of this essay, several books
by blacks have made the best seller list, including
Alex Haley's Roots.) According to Shockley, during
the twenty-five year period 1945-1970, only nine blacks
appeared on the best seller list and Frank Yerby
appeared nine times. She is perceptive in stating
that best sellers are not necessarily the best books
in literary value, that they are merely the books
that have the most sales. She establishes the fact
that Jessie Fauset, Zora Neale Hurston, Nella Larsen,
and Langston Hughes were just as good as writers as
Richard Wright when Black Boy became a best seller,
but that their books did not reach the best seller
lists. This statement leads her to assume "Black
writers can be made into best selling authors in the
same ways as whites. All this necessitates is that
publishers put forth more effort, time and money into
promoting their books." The weakness of the article

is its failure to mention the general criteria for inclusion on the best seller list and how these criteria have changed over the years.

A255.   "Black Librarians as Creative Writers." In Handbook of Black Librarianship 160-66.

Without introduction or conclusion, this informative essay lists eight black creative writers, four men and four women, who have had distinguished careers as librarians. These persons are Anne Spencer, Arna Bontemps, Oliver Austin Kirkpatrick, Dudley Randall, Leslie Morgan Collins, Ann Allen Shockley, Margaret Perry, and Sharon Bell Mathis. Chronologically arranged according to librarians' birthdates, these brief sketches include creative writings, awards received, and jobs each person has held as a librarian. This is Shockley's third essay in Handbook of Black Librarianship, and it appears under the heading "Significant Books and Periodicals for Black Collections." This piece seems misplaced. It would serve better under the heading "Afro-American Resources."

A256.   "A Descriptive Bibliography of Selected African and Afro-American Periodicals." In Handbook of Black Librarianship 143-52.

A selective descriptive bibliography, this list of sources contains thirty-six African and Afro-American periodicals of varied emphases. The list is intended to aid "librarians and educators in selecting basic titles for Afro-American collections and to supplement Black Studies curricula." The bibliography is a useful research tool; the entries include a brief note of each journal's relevance, the date the journal was founded, the frequency of publication, the mailing address, the editor, and the book's cost.

A257.   "Establishing Afro-American Collections." In Handbook of Black Librarianship 182-91.

Well written and meticulously researched, this article is an invaluable guide to all librarians wishing to establish an Afro-American collection. After citing Randall and Goodrich's definition of a "special collection" found in Principles of College Library Administration, Shockley proceeds to give criteria for the selection of books for an Afro-American collection. She suggests standard scholarly bibliographies as a means for starting the collection and cautions librarians about ordering books solely on the basis of book reviews. She encourages the ordering of such non-print materials as slides, cassettes, phono disks, films, and tapes, and includes the oral history interview as a good source for supplementing and complementing archival collections. Every archivist for Afro-American collections should read and digest this essay.

A258.   "The Role of the Curator of Afro-American Collections."
         In Handbook of Black Librarianship 192-202.

         Four fundamental tasks of the curator of Afro-American
         collections are listed and elaborated on. These are
         (1) collecting and preserving black materials,
         (2) making the materials available for use, (3) promo-
         ting scholarship and research, and (4) being an effi-
         cient and capable administrator. These tasks are noted
         as those undertaken by such well-known curators of
         Afro-American collections as Dorothy B. Porter, curator
         emeritus of the Moorland-Spingarn Research Center
         at Howard University, and Arthur A. Schomburg, founder
         and curator of the Schomburg Center for Research on
         Black Culture. For its details and advice, this is
         a centrally relevant and common sense essay.

A259.   "Oral History: A Research Tool for Black History."
         Negro History Bulletin 41 (Jan.-Feb. 1978): 787-89.

         The inestimable value of oral history in collecting
         and documenting black history is clearly emphasized
         here. As a research tool, it has supplemented written
         records that have been lost, stolen, or ignored; as
         history, it fills in the "missing pages" of the black
         experience in America. An unbiased scholar, Shockley
         gives the strengths and limitations of oral history
         and establishes criteria to evaluate the interview.
         This essay is must reading for a serious researcher
         of black history.

A260.   "The Black Lesbian in American Literature: An
         Overview." Conditions: Five (Autumn 1979): 133-42.
         Rpt. in Lesbian-Feminist Study Clearinghouse. Pitts-
         burgh: Women's Studies Program, of Pittsburgh, 1981.
         133-42. Also rpt. in Home Girls: A Black Feminist
         Anthology. Ed. Barbara Smith. New York: Kitchen Table-
         Women of Color P, 1983. 83-93. Also rpt. in Women
         Identified Women. Ed. Sandee Potter and Trudy Darty.
         Palo Alto: Mayfield, 1984. 267-75.

         That this is Shockley's only essay reprinted three
         times suggests its popularity on an unpopular and
         seldom written about subject -- the black lesbian.
         Reasons for the black lesbian's neglect in American
         literature range from black writers' concentrated
         desire to write about racism, to fear of being
         called lesbians, to publishers' indifference to
         works with lesbian themes. When black lesbians do
         appear in fiction, they are sketchily drawn, under-
         stated or derided, as in Maya Angelou's I Know Why
         a Caged Bird Sings and Gather Together in My Name,
         Gayle Jones' Corregidora and White Rat, Rosa Guy's
         Ruby, and Rita Mae Browns's In Her Day. Few essays
         have been written by and about black lesbians in
         literature, but among those existing Shockley highly
         regards Anita R. Cornwell's "The Black Lesbian in

a Malevolent Society." Shockley names black lesbian
poets and newspapers and concludes with a call for
more writings by black lesbians "to present another
side of the lives of Black women." This essay is good
for its sympathetic treatment of the black lesbian
issue.

A261.   "The Salsa Soul Sisters." Off Our Backs 9 (Nov. 1979):
13.

Shockley briefly introduces the Salsa Soul Sisters,
an organization of Third World gay women. Formed in
1976 by Reverend Dee Jackson, a black gay minister
who operates a prison ministry for Third World gay
women in Manhattan, the organization arrived at the
name "Salsa Soul Sisters" by combining the Spanish
word "Salsa" meaning "hot" with the black jargon
"soul." The function of the group is to articulate
problems and concerns of Third World gay women, who
meet at Washington Square Community Church in Greenwich
Village on Thursday nights. The group does not exclude
white members, but policy-making decisions are left
to Third World women. Information regarding the organization's newsletter and membership fees is given.
Exposure of a neglected group makes this an insightful
essay.

A262.   "Red Jordan Arobateau: A Different Kind of Black Lesbian Writer." Sinister Wisdom 21 (Fall 1982): 35-39.

Red Jordan Arobateau, the daughter of a Hondurus man
and a black American woman, is a relatively unknown,
unemployed writer who lives in Oakland, California,
with her twelve cats and two dogs. This essay highlights Arobateau's life. It gives an explanation for
her peculiar name, mentions her thirty-seven unpublished novels on gay and straight life, and relates
her inspiration for writing. Shockley learned about
Arobateau's works through Judy Grahn's True-to-Life
Adventure Stories, Vol. I; wanting to know more about
Arobateau, Shockley secured her telephone number from
a bookstore when purchasing Arobateau's self-published
novel, Bars across Heaven (1975). It is to Margaret
Cruikshank that Shockley owes a debt of gratitude
for driving her to Arobateau's home so that she might
meet the thirty-seven-year-old author. The information
gathered at this meeting is the essence of this essay.

A263.   "Black Lesbian Biography: Lifting the Veil." Other
Black Woman 1 (1982): 5-9.

Shockley's thesis is that while white women such as
Gertrude Stein, Vita Sachville-West, Emily Dickinson,
and Amy Lowell are recognized as lesbians by scholars,
black lesbians remain behind a veil. She affirms that
black lesbian foremothers did exist, despite the
attempts of biographers to separate the public lives

of black women from their private, sexual lives. She
cites several works supporting the fact that lesbian
relations (including marriages between women) did
exist and still do in Africa and that it is reasonable
to expect that some African women, brought to America
by slave traders, were lesbians. She identifies as
lesbians two black nineteenth century figures, Mary
Fields and Edmonia Lewis, both of whom wore men's
clothes. She concludes with a bow to Gloria Hull,
an energetic black scholar, who has lifted through
her research the veil concealing the lesbianism of
Alice Ruth Moore Dunbar-Nelson, wife of poet Paul
Laurence Dunbar.

A264. "On Lesbian/Feminist Book Reviewing." Sojourner: The
       Women's Forum 9 (Apr. 1984): 18.

This article asserts that too many mediocre reviewers
examine and write about lesbian/feminist books. These
reviewers fall short of excellence for several reasons:
lack of adequate time spent on book reviewing, poor
background book knowledge, inexperience, and shoddy
literary commentary. Shockley insists that "a review
should delineate the author's background, purpose,
style, writing abilities, and success in fulfilling
her aims." She then ridicules two reviews of her novel
Say Jesus and Come to Me because one reviewer care-
lessly mistakes her as a white woman and the other
ignorantly denies the existence of the black experience
in the novel. The essay's essential usefulness is
its listing the five requirements for criticizing
a book and its identifying publications which present
good reviews of lesbian/feminist works. These publications include Backbone, Feminary, Frontiers, Gay
Community News, New Women's Times, Signs, Sojourner,
and Women's Review of Books.

A265. "Black Book Collections: Quality Verses Quantity."
       Unpublished essay, 1974.

Deploring the poor quality of many books published
on the black experience since the 1960's, Shockley
declares, "I would rather see one good work published
than ten weak ones, for exploitive gain." The proli-
feration of books on blacks has contributed, she
notes, to librarians' buying books of poor academic
quality. She, therefore, lists reputable references
to consult as guides for choosing books. The high
point of the essay is her discussion of the limited
review avenues for black books, the check points to
use in determining good book reviews, and her plea
to blacks to review black books in white journals.

A266. "The Rationale and Technique for Processing the
       Interview." Unpublished essay, 1975.

The techniques and steps used for processing the oral
history interview are clearly explained. The essay

emphasizes meticulousness of details to ensure accuracy of the transcription. A primary value of the essay is the listing of references in which the holdings of Fisk University's oral history collections are published.

A267.   "Oral History and the Archives Program at Fisk University." Unpublished essay, 1976.

Included in Fisk University's historical background is its distinction as "the first black institution to become a member of the Society of American Archivists." As a major black archives, Fisk University's Archives Division houses over sixty collections which include the original works of W.E.B. Du Bois, Fisk Jubilee Singers, Charles Chesnutt, and Jean Toomer. Fisk's archives also has tapes on oral history which fill in the gaps of black history that has been lost or destroyed. The importance of an archival collection to a people's culture is stressed in this essay.

A268.   "Black History Month: A Reappraisal." Unpublished essay, 1979.

A reappraisal of Black History Month reveals that it is as much needed now as it was in 1915, when black historian Carter G. Woodson initiated the event as a means of celebrating the contributions of black Americans. An interesting revelation is that the lack of concern for black writings exhibited by large publishers has contributed immensely to the need for Black History Month.

A269.   "Oral History for Genealogy Research." Unpublished essay, 1979.

Oral history is important to family research because it collects and preserves past information that "might be lost by the death of a relative." The essay proceeds with ways to conduct the interview and how to transcribe the tape. Important to the discussion is the reminder that legal forms should be signed by interviewer and interviewee for the protection of both.

A270.   "The Black Lesbian: Invisible Woman in American Literature." Unpublished essay, 1979.

The invisibility of the black lesbian in black literature, writes Shockley, stems primarily from the homophobic attitude of the black community. This attitude prevents many black writers from treating lesbian themes for fear of exclusion from the black community, family, and literary circles. Consequently, at the time Shockley wrote this essay, only two novels existed that had been written by blacks about the black lesbian-- Shockley's Loving Her (1974) and Rosa Guy's Ruby (1976). The appearance of the black lesbian in the works of white writers is just as infrequent;

she appears briefly in Rita Mae Brown's _In Her Day_
(1976) and Jane DeLynn's _Some Do_ (1978). Further analysis of the absence of the black lesbian in American
poetry, criticism, and anthologies offers a neglected
aspect of American life that needs attention.

A271.   "Third World Lesbian/Feminist Writing and Publishing:
         A Pragmatic View." Unpublished essay, 1980.

         Shockley's pragmatic view of Third World lesbian/
         feminist writing and publishing is very grim. She
         sees few opportunities for unknown black women writers
         to publish their works, owing to fewer demands for
         black studies courses, dwindling federal money, the
         formation and merging of publishing conglomerates,
         and the fact that the majority of black people do
         not buy books. She offers four suggestions to the
         lesbian/feminist writer who wishes to publish: print
         works privately, get the imprint of a vanity press,
         submit works to small, independent lesbian/feminist
         publishers, and support the founding of a Third World
         lesbian press. Despite publishing setbacks for the
         lesbian/feminist writers, Shockley urges them to con-
         tinue writing.

A272.   "Introduction to Filmstrip, History of an All-Black
         Town: Mound Bayou, Mississippi." Unpublished essay,
         1981.

         The filmstrip on Mound Bayou, Mississippi documents
         the story of a black Montgomery family, slaves to
         Joseph Davis, and its pursuit of an all-black utopian
         community. The purpose of the filmstrip is to reveal
         "how oral history interviews, along with archival
         and manuscript collection materials, can be combined
         and utilized as a visual concept for documenting
         history." Approximately thirty minutes in length,
         the filmstrip is an amateurish experiment. This essay
         on the filmstrip makes the salient point that produc-
         tion of a filmstrip requires financial backing.

A273.   "On Writing and Writers." Unpublished essay, 1982.

         Shockley begins by dispelling the erroneously-held
         notion that published writers make a lot of money.
         She names several black writers, including herself,
         who have to work to earn a living. She refers to a
         1979 study of the Author's Guild Foundation of 2,239
         writers, conducted by the Columbia Center for Social
         Sciences, that revealed the medium income of the
         writers to be $4,777 annually.

         Shockley then discusses the climate for black writers
         in the 1970's and 1980's, focusing on the difficulty
         black writers have in getting their works published.
         She views this difficulty as stemming primarily from
         the takeover of publishing houses by monopolies and
         conglomerates whose major concern is publishing the

book that will sell. Despite the difficulties writers encounter, Shockley says she continues to write because "Writing is a compulsion with me." She reveals the times she writes and the inspiration for her writing. This essay is important for Shockley's personal views about the state of writing in general and her disclosures about her specific works, such as "The More Things Change," "Crying for Her Man," and A Love So Bold.

A274.   "Black Women's History Resources in the Fisk University Library's Black Oral History Collection." Unpublished essay, 1982.

A National Endowment for the Humanities grant strengthened black women's history resources in Fisk University Library's Black Oral History Collection. The grant enabled the employment of full-time staff and the taping of more than five hundred interviews, many of which with women. These interviews with black women include physicians (Drs. Helen O. Dickens and Barbara Wright), lawyers (Jewel La Fontant and Edith Sampson), educators (Dr. Willa Player and Inez Smith Reid), feminists (Aileen Hernandez and Angela Davis), politicians (Delores Tucker), editors (Marcia Gillespie), and literary figures (Nikki Giovanni, Margaret Walker). White women involved with black life were also interviewed, including Greta Park Redfield, daughter of sociologist Robert Park who taught at Fisk; and Catherine Jones Gaskell, daughter of Fisk University's white ex-president, Thomas Elsa Jones. A total of 114 women were interviewed from May 1970 to March 1974. This essay documents the continued strength of Fisk University Library as a repository of resources on black life.

A275.   "On Afro-American Women Writers and Writing." Unpublished essay, 1985.

Shockley regards Afro-American women writers as foremothers who gave birth to Afro-American literature. These women were the first black poets, the first to publish a book, a book of poems, a novel, a collection of essays, a short story, and a biography. These and other early black women writers have been eclipsed by male writers of the Harlem Renaissance. However, since the 1940's, these black writers, according to Shockley, have been receiving more recognition for their works. They are winning literary prizes, receiving reviews in New York Times, and establishing their own newspapers. The appeal of this essay is its compilation of relevant facts in overviewing the black woman writer for the last two centuries.

BOOK REVIEWS

A276.   Night Riders in Folk History, by Gladys-Marie Fry.
Oral History Newsletter Fall 1973: 3.

Points out that Night Riders in Black Folk History
"fills a gap in black history by supplying fresh
historical evidence through the hardly tapped resource
of the black oral tradition." Chief among the new
information that Shockley cites Fry as bringing to
light are slave informants' descriptions of the patty
rollers' dress and their sadistic and lawless actions
which discount previously published accounts of the
antebellum patrollers as "discreet and sober men."
Also coming out of the black folk reminiscences of
the patty rollers is their reflection on the black
folk hero "who outwitted various systems of control."
Shockley reiterates the importance of oral history
used in this study; relying on storytelling from
generation to generation, oral history has preserved
another phase of neglected black culture.

A277.   Index to Black Poetry, by Dorothy H. Chapman. American
Reference Books Annual 7 (1976): 584.

Cites Chapman's Index to Black Poetry as the "first-
of-its-kind index." As such, it has two major limitations: It draws most of its information from two
of Dorothy Porter's bibliographies, thereby limiting
its scope considerably; and it indexes "primarily
collected works and pamphlets by individual poets
instead of anthologies." Despite these flaws, Shockley
still views the work as "an important and needed
guide to black poetry."

A278.   Claiming an Identity They Taught Me to Despise, by
Michelle Cliff. Azalea 4 (Spring-Summer 1981): 16-
17.

Posits that the motif of passing, a long-time theme
in Afro-American literature, "breaks new ground"
in Michelle Cliff's book. A Jamaican born of "white-
looking parents" and sent to England to study the
Italian Renaissance, Cliff embarks on a journey to
find the black heritage "visible in the dark skin
of her great-grandfather." Five chapters of wandering,
previously appearing in other publications, make
for a disjointedness that Shockley views as the work's
sole weakness. This flaw is minimized, however, by
the book's evocative language and keen perception.

A279.   Gifts of Power: The Writings of Rebecca Jackson,
Black Visionary, Shaker, Eldress, ed. Jean McMahon
Humez. Tennessean [Nashville] 16 Jan. 1983: F4.

Praises the book as "a testament to the courage and
strength of a woman who...broke away from traditional
restraints to attain self-fullment." Rebecca Jackson,
born free in Philadelphia in 1795, left her husband

and the AME Church to join the Shakers and adhere to a theology of celibacy, spiritualism, and feminism. Disenchanted with the Shakers' attitude toward blacks, she left the security of the Shaker community in Watervliet, New York and started a black Shaker sisterhood in Philadelphia, where she dispersed spiritual blessings to slave and free blacks. Jean McMahon Humez's "interpretative introduction," which provides an informative background to Jackson's writings, makes the book all the more relevant, asserts Shockley.

A280.   "Black Women's 'Double Jeopardy' Probed." Rev. of We Are Your Sisters: Black Women in the Nineteenth Century, ed. Dorothy Sterling. Tennessean [Nashville] 2 Sept. 1984: D10.

Compares Dorothy Sterling's We Are Your Sisters with Gerda Lerner's Black Women in White America. Both are documentary histories, but, of the two, Shockley decidedly favors Sterling's work because it presents the "intimate and the personal, which best portray the black woman's interior world." Of especial appeal to Shockley is Sterling's use of examples (washerwomen striking for $1.50 a day in Jackson, Mississippi in 1866) to document injustices against black women. Sterling, a white woman, does "not try to conceal her admiration and respect for the black women in her book."

A281.   "Diary Enriches Black Women's Literature." Rev. of Give Us Each Day: The Diary of Alice Dunbar-Nelson, ed. Gloria T. Hull. Tennessean [Nashville] 13 Oct. 1985: F10.

Regards Hull's Give Us Each Day as "another salient work in Afro-American women's literature." Shockley draws from this work varied facets of Alice Moore Dunbar-Nelson's life. Beginning her humble existence in New Orleans, Louisiana, Dunbar-Nelson became the wife of nationally acclaimed poet Paul Laurence Dunbar, participated in national black conventions and women's clubs, and garnered recognition for her-self as writer, suffragette, and anti-lynching crusader. She had the cultural behavior of the well-to-do, but could "get down with the 'roughnecky' and enjoy 'black market Italian red wine and bootleg whiskey.'" It is Hull's treatment of the totality of Dunbar-Nelson's experiences that kindles Shockley's interest in and admiration for this work of valuable scholarship.

A282.   "Role of Female Slave Given Full Treatment." Rev. of Ar'n't I a Woman? by Deborah Gray White. Tennessean [Nashville] 22 June 1986: F9.

Views this study as "the first attempt to deal ex-clusively with the status of black female slaves in the South." As such, it derives its title from

the famous speech of ex-slave Sojourner Truth,
delivered to the Woman's Rights Convention of 1851.
The study inspects the various myths related to black
women slaves, examines the conditions and attitudes
of female slaves, and scrutinizes child care and
family structure of slaves. Shockley approves of
the work's readability, but dismisses it as not providing "any startlingly new information."

LIBRARY BOOKS

A283.   Living   Black   American   Authors: A   Biographical
         Directory. Ed. Ann Allen Shockley and Sue P. Chandler.
         New York: Bowker, 1973.

         Shockley   states   in   the   Preface   that   "the   paucity
         of   information   about   living   black   American   authors
         led   to   the   compilation   of   this   work."   It   is   her   re-
         cognition   of   a   need   and   fulfilling   it   that   makes
         this   work   a   valuable   contribution   to   modern   scholar-
         ship.   It   is   a   pioneer   work   and   understandably   has
         flaws   inherently   borne   in   the   difficult   manner   in
         which   the   materials   had   to   be   collected;   the   dif-
         ficulty   in   compiling   the   materials   is   mentioned   in
         the Preface.

         The   directory   consists   of   more   than   four   hundred
         entries   of   living   black   American   authors.   Biographical
         data   include   place   of   birth,   education,   family,   pro-
         fessional   experience,   awards,   publications,   and
         mailing   address;   the   data   format,   however,   is   not
         consistent   for   each   biographee.   Some   minor   writers
         such   as   Mignon   Holland   Anderson   and   Cleo   Overstreet
         (now   deceased)   are   excluded;   some   major   writers   are
         omitted,   too.   In   fact,   the   omission   of   George   S.
         Schuyler   prompted   him   to   write   a   very   caustic   review
         of   the   book   in   the   Union   Leader   newspaper.   A   list
         of   black   publishers   and   a   title   index   follow   the
         entries for biographees.

         Despite   its   omissions,   this   directory   puts   blacks
         and   whites   in   contact   with   America's   difficult-to-
         locate   black   writers   and   publishers.   It   has   been
         of   considerable   service   to   many   since   its   publication.
         The   first   of   its   kind,   R. R. Bowker   rushed   Shockley
         and Chandler to publish it.

A284.   Handbook of Black Librarianship. Comp. and Ed. E.J.
         Josey   and   Ann   Allen   Shockley.   Littleton: Libraries
         Unlimited, 1977.

         Handbook of Black Librarianship is,   as   the   editors
         indicate,   a   useful   tool   not   only   for   librarians,
         teachers,   and   scholars,   but   also   for   students,   book-
         sellers,   and   publishers.   Its   importance   lies   in   the
         accomplished   objectives   set   forth   by   Josey   and   Shock-
         ley   in   the   Introduction: (1)   it   "fills   a   void   for
         a   variety   of   people   needing   Afro-American   and   African
         materials   and   information   on   the   location   of   these
         materials...;   (2)   it   preserves   the   heritage   of   blacks
         in   librarianship   and   chronicles   current   thinking
         among   Afro-American   librarians...;and   (3)   it   seeks
         to   serve   all   people   by   identifying   those   materials

essential to an African/Afro-American collection
(large and small) by providing information on black
publishers and their specializations, by identifying
selected bookstores specializing in African and Afro-
American materials, by identifying those libraries
...that serve predominantly black populations, and
by instructing them as to how to establish and maintain archives and special collections." Several years
of work went into the completion of this book which
became a labor of love for the two black veteran
librarians working at predominantly black university
libraries.

This reference book is divided into seven unevenly
distributed sections with thirty-seven entries (not
all essays) of varying lengths. Together, these
entries trace the history of black librarianship
in this country from the early nineteenth century
to the present, focus on vital issues pertaining
to black librarianship, and offer pertinent suggestions regarding Afro-American and American resources.
The remaining one hundred pages are devoted to
reference lists including "Undergraduate Library
School Departments in Predominantly Black Colleges
and Universities." A useful Index is also provided.

As comprehensive as this reference is, questions
arise regarding choice of certain materials: What
criteria were used for the inclusion of African resources? Why is one section of the book devoted to
African resources and none to Carribean resources?
Why is the section "Vital Issues in Black Librarianship" overweighted with three essays on black children
and not one esay on the critical importance for black
libraries to preserve the local history of blacks
born and bred in the state in which the black library
is located? In the latter instance, an essay about
how to establish an archival collection on a state's
black history would have enhanced considerably this
section.

Other questions regarding the placement and omission
of material are in order: Why is the essay "Black
Librarians as Creative Writers" placed under the
heading "Significant Books and Periodicals for Black
Collectors" and not under, say, "Afro-American Resources"? Why are the last one hundred pages set
off from the rest of the text instead of included
under the broad heading "Afro-American Resources"?
Why is the famed Collis P. Huntington Library at
Hampton University omitted from the list of black
academic libraries in Virginia?

These questions neither deny the relevance of this
reference book nor argue against its usefulness to
those for whom it was intended. In fact, the American
public would suffer a considerable loss if subsequent
editions of The Handbook of Black Librarianship were

not published. Its relevance is evident by its having been nominated for the 1978 Ralph R. Shaw Award as an outstanding contribution to library literature.

A285.   A History of Public Library Services to Negroes in the South, 1900-1955. Dover: Delaware State College, 1959 (Unpublished monograph).

This monograph gives an overview of public library service to Negroes in thirteen Southern states from 1900 to 1955. The study reveals that public library service to Negroes in the South was slow, sporadic, and segregated. From 1903 when Charlotte, North Carolina, established the first independent Negro library until 1954, when the Supreme Court handed down its desegregation decision, the majority of Negroes in the South did without public library service.

A286.   A Handbook for the Administration of Special Black Collections. 3rd ed. Nashville: Fisk University, 1974 (Unpublished monograph).

The third revision and enlargement of a handbook that was printed first in 1970 and again in 1971, this edition "was prepared for the Mini-Institute in Research Services in Black Studies Librarianship." It aids librarians in organizing and servicing black black collections. Divided into seven sections, it includes such items as staff administration, lists of black periodicals, newspapers, audio-visual materials, and sources of manuscript and archival materials on Afro-American culture.

III.
REVIEWS OF SHOCKLEY'S
FICTION AND NONFICTION

REVIEWS OF "A MEETING OF THE SAPPHIC DAUGHTERS"

B1. Eleanor. Response to Ann Allen Shockley's "A Meeting
     of the Sapphic Daughters." <u>Sinister Wisdom</u> 11 (Fall
     1979): 56-59.

     Outlines eleven reasons Eleanor can identify with racism
     among lesbians occurring in Shockley's short story,
     "A Meeting of the Sapphic Daughters." Eleanor, like
     the characters Patrice and Lettie, knows what racism
     looks like, and feels like, and where it comes from,
     and suggests that Shockley did not offer a solution
     to it in this short story because "it isn't resolved
     now [in real life] -- and won't be."

     Preceding Eleanor's response, the editors of <u>Sinister</u>
     <u>Wisdom</u> announce that they are printing letters, never
     intended for publication, "as a first step toward sharing
     information in <u>Sinister Wisdom</u> about how racism manifests
     itself among lesbians -- what it looks like, what it
     feels like, where it comes from, and how to stop it."

B2. Schwarz, Judith. Response to Ann Allen Shockley's "A
     Meeting of the Sapphic Daughters." <u>Sinister Wisdom</u> 11
     (Fall 1979): 59-60.

     Relates the racial ostracism portrayed in "A Meeting
     of the Sapphic Daughters" to that which occurred during
     the 1960's Daughters of Bilitis meetings she attended
     in San Francisco. She remembers black, chicana, and
     Chinese lesbians attending one meeting but never return-
     ing, and the whites never attempting to find out why.
     Schwarz then makes a connection between the ostracism
     exhibited toward third world women at these meetings
     and her own ostracism by educated people "because I
     wasn't educated at the time...." Praising Shockley's

story as "a very thought provoking, strong story, Schwarz concludes with an angry question: "Will we ever get past all the garbage in our heads we grew up hearing and unthinkingly incorporating into our beliefs?"

B3. Gubar, Susan. "Sapphistries." <u>Signs</u> 10 (Autumn 1984): 43-62.

Cites Shockley's "Meeting of the Sapphic Daughters" as one example of a piece by a modern writer exhibiting distrust of Sappho; Shockley's short story "uncovers the implicit racism of elitist Sapphic cults." Other modern writers named are Rita Mae Brown, Muriel Rukeyser, Sylvia Plath, and Robin Morgan. Gubar traces the influence of Sappho on ancient and modern writers and notes that one reason for modern writers' distrust of Sappho is her ambiguous life (she committed suicide because of her unrequited love for Phaon), according to Ovid's version.

REVIEWS OF THE BLACK AND WHITE OF IT

B4. White, Gayle. Motherroot Journal 2 (Summer 1980): 4.

Singles out The Black and White of It as "a thoughtful
well-crafted collection of stories." Among Shockley's
strengths are character, dialogue, and human-dilemma
emphasis. Despite the conventional situations and pre-
dictable endings, White regards this collection "as
an outstanding piece" in "the restricted field of lesbian
fiction."

B5. K., Elizabeth. Atalanta 8 (August 1980): 2-3.

Reviews Paula Christian's Love Is Where You Find It
(Timely Books) with Ann Shockley's The Black and White
of It and prefers the latter because the stories are
not all contemporary, the characters are not all white,
and they do not engage in "explicit sex." It is Shockley's avoidance of "this massive trend" that enables
The Black and the White of It to gain this reviewer's
acceptance.

B6. Norris, Maryel. Plexus 7 (Sept. 1980): 17.

Attests that The Black and White of It is "highly readable and very much to the point." Norris is especially
attracted to the challenges which Shockley's characters
face, but hastens to add that these "characters are
not as militant or movement-oriented as the 'out' black
lesbians of the 1970's... but [they do] portray the
weight of triple jeopardy in our society, being Black,
a woman, and a lesbian."

B7. Feola, Dorothy. Women's Newsletter Network 9 (Fall
1980): 14-16.

Reviews Marge Piercy's The Moon Is Always Female (a
collection of poems) with Ann Allen Shockley's The Black
and White of It and regards both as "The best of...
books." Feola especially admires Shockley's third person
narrator, the use of flashbacks, and plot brevity.

B8. McKay, Nellie. "Ground Breaking for Black Lesbians:
The Black and White of It." Bread and Roses 2 (Autumn
1980): 43.

Includes The Black and White of It with other groundbreaking scholarly contributions related to black women.
McKay commends Shockley for facing "head-on" in her
short stories the problems encountered by black and
white lesbians in interracial and intraracial relationships and for articulating the theme of "human vulnerability" among these women. Shockley's portrayal of these
experiences demonstrates her "expertise as a good crafts-
woman" and the sensitivity of "one who really cares
about the conditions of women's lives...."

B9.   Patton, Cynthia. "Woman Bonding." Sojourner 6 (Nov.
       1980): 15-16.

       Reviews Jan Clausen's Mother, Sister, Daughter, Lover
       and Shockley's The Black and White of It. Patton sees
       both works dealing primarily with those women who "do
       not or cannot draw on male privilege," employing a
       wide range of characters, and treating their characters
       struggling in a world whose attitudes and strictures
       need to be dropped. Shockley's characters especially
       exhibit the pain of having to make "decisions between
       people, between heritages, between our loved ones and
       our place in the world."

B10.   White, Evelyn C. WLW Journal 5 (Nov.-Dec. 1980): 12-
       13.

       Claims that The Black and White of It "further develops
       the racial themes...first dealt with in Loving Her.
       Sexual self-denial or sexual sacrifice is the most
       prominent theme demonstrated in such stories as "Play
       It, But Don't Say It" and "The Play." White contends
       that despite some flaws in the presentation of themes,
       this collection of short stories "affirms the reality
       and dignity of lesbian lives."

B11.   De Veaux, Alexis. 13th Moon 5.1-2 (1981): 144.

       Contends that most of Shockley's characters have no
       depth. Except for the women in the stories "Home to
       Meet the Folks" and "A Birthday Remembered," there
       is something "neurotic" and "ever-tragic" in the women's
       lives. They are "victims of their sexuality," which
       De Veaux considers "an outdated mode of thought." They
       hasten from sad situations with men to sadder circum-
       stances with women. The women's inability to express
       true love emphatically distracts from the "art" that
       should have been the core of this collection.

B12.   Koppelman, Susan. "Ann Allen Shockley." Critical Survey
       of Short Fiction: Current Writers. 7 Vols. Ed. Frank
       N. Magill. Englewood Cliffs: Salem P, 1981. 7: 2814.

       Views Shockley's The Black and White of It as concerned
       with how "the lives of individual and coupled black
       heterosexuals and black and racially unidentified
       lesbians are short circuited by racism, sexism, and
       homophobia." Koppelman sees considerable tension in
       these short stories which document "the erosion of
       hope, the challenges to loyalty ... the insecurities
       of those trapped in socially devalued categories, and
       the poisoning of love and intimacy by the invasion
       of bigotry."

B13.   Cornell, Michiyo. "Racism and Homophobia Explored."
       Gay Insurgent 36 (Spring 1981): 36-37.

       Admires this collection of short stories for the various
       themes (racism, homophobia, and rejection) exhibited.

What Cornell does not like about the book is its focus
being limited to black and white characters and its
implication that "lesbians don't have or shouldn't
want children except as part of being trapped in the
straight world."

B14. T., Sharon. <u>Lesbian Voices</u> 4.1 (1981): 15-16.

Proclaims this work as "signalling a new era of honesty
in discussing the lesbian community's problems." Shockley exposes the myths that "black lesbians do not exist"
and that "lesbianism is a white conspiracy to achieve
black genocide." Sharon T. does not agree that all
the couples have a "fantastic" sex life, but she does
feel that "sexual dissatisfaction" among lesbian characters will not be admitted by any writer until "lesbian
sex is socially approved as a valid alternative."

B15. Reynolds, Lynne. "The Black and White of It."
      <u>Conditions: Seven</u> 3 (Spring 1981): 152-58.

Describes the stories as "flat," written according
to a repetitious "formula" and void of "potentially
volatile interactions" that the reader anticipates.
Reynolds became "angry" when reading these stories
because Shockley seemed to have drawn the characters
"from a two-dimensional universe, inhabiting a world
charged with negativism." All the characters exhibit
life as "difficult" and "painful," and in all the
stories characterizations are "shadowy and insubstan-
tial." Reynolds says the stories reflect the 1950's
rather than a "contemporary time sense" because of
the absence of the influence of the gay liberation
and women's movements and because of restricted choices
the women make. As a lesbian, Reynolds is unable to
identify "with the characters in the stories."

B16. Gingerlox. <u>Lesbian</u> 3 (Apr. 1981): N. pag.

Points out that Shockley employs "characters...in situations where most of us can identify." Gingerlox particularly identifies with the characters in "Love Motion"
because this story "validates" a theory she has long
held: "That for some women, the only way they can
tolerate heterosex is to fantasize about making love
with another woman." She credits Shockley with unbiased
delineations of blacks and whites.

B17. T., Sharon. <u>Lambda News</u> 6 (13 Apr. 1981): N. pag.

Reprint of review found in <u>Lesbian Voices</u> 4.1 (1981):
15-16.

B18. Jay, Karla. "Deny, Deny, Deny." <u>New Women's Times
      Feminist Review</u> 15 (Apr.-May 1981): 17-18.

Uses Rita B. Dandridge's article "Male Critics/Black
Women's Novels" as a springboard to the discussion
of Shockley's works and the generally poor reception

she has received for her lesbian fiction. (Jay even
mentions that in her review of Loving Her, appearing
in WIN magazine December 1974, the "editors snipped
out the positive comments and left in the bad ones".)
That Shockley continues to write in the face of such
reception "is a testament to her courage and a blessing
to the rest of us." Regarding The Black and White of
It as a better work than Loving Her, Jay sees in the
short stories genuine honesty, fuller character delineations, and the development of three realistic
themes -- ageism, homoerotaphobia, and racism. The
book is regarded as a groundbreaker, and Kay warns
that "one can either face up to the problems [contained
therein] and to reality -- or deny, deny, deny."

B19.   Morris, Debra. Off Our Backs 11 (Oct. 1981): 16.

Sees the "closet" as omnipresent in Shockley's stories.
It not only keeps the characters safe, but also announces their self-denial. It bespeaks of a violence
(unlike that in Loving Her) inherent in "a passive
belief of many of the characters that they are entitled
to life's small portions."

B20.   Mushroom, Merril. Feminary 1 (1982): 152-61.

Says these stories are about the lives of lesbians
who lived during the 1950's. As a backdrop to a discussion of Shockley's characters, Mushroom recalls
the Charlie John investigations of the 1950's which
purged Florida's university campuses of "lesbian and
homosexual faculty and students," among whom Mushroom
could be found with others, caught and humiliated.
It is the secrecy of lesbians' lives that Shockley
writes about that Mushroom identifies with and says
might be "distasteful...to some modern-day lesbians."
Shockley's women are privileged, career-oriented
persons, but their circumstances are similar to those
of the lesbians Mushroom knew in the 1950's. What is
missing in the lives of Shockley's characters, writes
Mushroom, are "the blackmail and extortion attempts,
the buying of temporary safety from exposure as a queer
by someone who knew."

B21.   Cruikshank, Margaret, ed. Lesbian Studies: Present
and Future. Old Westbury: Feminist P, 1982. 59, 103,
107, 147, 151.

Regards The Black and White of It as recommended reading
in women's studies courses, but adds that it is debatable whether the short story collection is feminist
fiction or not.

B22.   Scruggs-Rodgers, Emma. Sepia 31 (Mar. 1982): 38.

Regards this collection as "an important work about
women loving women from the black perspective." Its
forte is that it allows readers to "broaden their
awareness" about women-bonding relationships.

B23.   Lundberg, Chris. <u>Lammas Little Review</u> 3 (Spring 1983):
       7-8.

       Thanks Ann Allen Shockley "for again sharing with us
       the lives of women some of us don't often get a chance
       to know." The women Lundberg refers to are those who
       deny and affirm their lesbianism. The two stories Lund-
       berg likes least because of the characters' denial
       of themselves as lesbians are "The Play" and "Love
       Motion"; the two she likes best are "A Birthday
       Remembered" and "A Special Evening."

B24.   Bright, Joyce. "Between the Covers." <u>The Word Is Out</u>
       (n.d): N. pag.

       Praises Shockley's collection. In fact, Bright says
       "I can't praise these stories enough." The concise
       writing, the tension "that portrays human emotions,"
       and the progression from one story to another are what
       make this collection "humanistic writing at its best!"

REVIEWS OF LOVING HER

B25.   Unsigned. Kirkus Review 42 (15 May 1974): 552-53.

Declares that Loving Her contains a "Victorian-
esque retribution of death" which conflicts with
its "dogmatic 'up' tone." The reviewer also sees
as incongruent the protagonist's "hyperbolic elegies
of...devotion" and "the so-called promiscuity for
every other gay character."

B26.   Unsigned. Publishers' Weekly 205 (20 May 1974):
59.

Views Loving Her as a sincere work in portraying
"the beauty, drama and frustration of love on the
fringes of society," but regards it as devoting
excessive attention to "domestic trivia." It is
labelled a "woman's novel."

B27.   Smothers, Joyce W. Library Journal 99 (Aug. 1974):
1986.

Condemns the work as "so stridently pro-liberation
that it resembles a polemic more than a novel"
and charges it is "not worth defending to your
strait-laced borrowers."

B28.   Unsigned. New Womankind 2 (Sept. 1974): 7.

Reviews Loving Her favorably. It is "a beautiful
story between a Black and white woman which deals
with sexism in the Black community, racism in the
white community, and the triple vulnerability of
a woman who is Black, lesbian, and female."

B29.   Cordova, Jeanne. Lesbian Tide 4 (Oct. 1974): 18.

Contends that "the bromidic narration of Loving
Her makes this potentially beautiful story difficult
to believe or enjoy." Among the chief aspects cited
as contributing to the narrative's dullness are
faulty characterization, a sophomoric literary
style, hackneyed scenes, and excessive propagan-
dizing. Cordova rates Shockley's novel low on every
aspect imaginable, but she does regard highly
two other novels about lesbianism, Patience and
Sarah and Ruby Fruit Jungle.

B30.   SunCircle, Patti. So's Your Old Lady 6 (Nov. 1974):
23.

Considers Loving Her the "first book" about "the
black lesbian experience." As such, SunCircle identifies with it and accepts it for not being "chocked
full of psychological interpretations, political
rhetoric and condemnations." Her regret is that

Shockley's novel will probably not be viewed in
<u>Essence</u> because of that magazine's "policy of
heterosexual fanaticism."

B31. Jay, Karla. <u>WIN</u> 12 (Dec. 1974): 20.

Takes the position that <u>Loving Her</u> does not reflect
the views and attitudes of "most movement dykes"
because the major characters "commit all the deadly
sins we preach so vehemently against." In very
illustrative language, Jay sketches the four sins
the novel commits: (1) "Thou shalt not play roles,"
(2) "Thou shalt not commit monogamy," (3) "Thou
shall not commit classism," and (4) "Thou shall
always present the 'correct' image of dykedom in
the media." Although Jay does not always give
correct information about the characters' actions,
her review is one of the most insightful regarding
this novel's position in the realm of dykedom.
She suggests preserving the book because it does
have "an overwhelming sense of reality" in its
reflections of a "middle-class forties generation
of lesbians," it presents an "unusual and perceptive
study of an interracial relationship," and the
author's style shows promise.

B32. Gohdes, Jackie. <u>Gold Flower Newspaper</u> 6 (Feb.
1975): 6,7.

Posits the novel's central theme as "the validity
of love overcoming the hatred, fear, and poverty
too common in our world." To achieve her theme,
Shockley depicts loving individuals with basically
a positive attitude about life. Despite Shockley's occasional lapses into triteness, Gohdes
regards this novel as coming the "closest to
ringing true in the descriptions of [the characters'] tenderest moments together."

B33. Unsigned. <u>Village Voice</u> 24 Mar. 1975: 17.

Quotes Alice Walker's statement regarding <u>Loving
Her</u>: "To my knowledge, <u>Loving Her</u> is the first
novel about an interracial lesbian relationship
written by a black woman." Walker's statement,
no doubt, reflects the manner in which <u>Village
Voice</u> regards Ann Shockley's novel.

B34. Walker, Alice. "A Daring Subject Boldly Shared."
<u>MS</u>. 2 (Apr. 1975): 120, 124.

Refers to <u>Loving Her</u> as "the first novel about
an interracial lesbian relationship written by
a black woman." Its importance is that "it enables
us to see and understand...the choices certain
women have made about how they will live their
lives...and allows us glimpses at physical inti-
macies between women...[previously] ridiculed

or obscured." Walker regards the characters as
being not fully developed but says the novel's
exploration of "a daring subject boldly shared"
allows readers "a new way of seeing and caring."

B35. Stanley, Julia P. "Uninhibited Angels: Metaphors
for Love." Margins 23 (Aug. 1975): 7-10.

Reviews Loving Her along with a dozen other lesbian
novels written before and after 1970. The lesbian
character in novels before the 1970's, posits
Stanley, is "so guilt-ridden by her identity" that
she "transcends her depravity and attains a strained
spirituality through her self-denial and mutila-
tion"; in so doing, she approaches "sainthood in
the eyes of the Outside World through her Fall."
The characters in lesbian novels after 1970 are
presented as human beings "standing firmly on
whatever ground we can claim." Loving Her, published
after 1970, uses the plot structure of the earlier
novels, and Stanley regards this use of structure
a weakness in Loving Her.

B36. Phillips, Frank Lamont. Black World 24 (Sept.
1975): 89-90.

Characterizes Loving Her as a "shabby example"
of Shockley's craft. Shockley is accused of "pro-
selytizing" and "lying" in her depiction of
Jerome Lee as "so purely physical and stupid" and
his wife Renay as "so good." What Phillips is most
piqued about is the "racial angle" the novel takes,
and he questions, "Has anyone besides this reviewer
noticed how many white lovers populate the Black
imagination?" The work so infuriated Phillips that
he signs off by saying, "This bullshit should not
be encouraged."

B37. Crew, Louie. WIN 20 May 1976: 10.

Considers Loving Her a serious novel. Crew considers
it "artful enough to focus clearly on Gay pain
and Gay weakness, politically honest enough to
understand Gay and Black vulnerability."

B38. Unsigned. Publishers' Weekly 213 (1 May 1978):
83.

Reprints PW's May 20 1974 review.

B39. Smith, Beverly. Gay Community News 6 (11 Nov. 1978),
Book Supplement: 4,8.

Attests that Loving Her makes an important political
declaration: "Black lesbians do exist and therefore
racism is a vital issue for lesbian communities
and homophobia and sexism are vital issue for
black communities." Despite this essential state-

ment, Smith believes the reader "is constantly
jarred by contraditions [in the novel]" because
Shockley lacks lesbian feminist analysis." One
such contradiction is Shockley's blending an attack
on marriage through Jerome Lee's description of
his wife as his "property" with an acceptance of
the marriage institution in Renay's assumption
of the roles of mother and cook, while Terry, her
lover, assumes the roles of father and husband.
Flaws aside, Loving Her satisfies Smith's "deep
hunger for images" of lesbians.

B40. Clark, Terri. Off Our Backs 9 (Nov. 1979): 21.

Asserts that Loving Her was written years before
the public read it because Shockley "struggled
for a long time to get it published." She views
information contained in it as predating "the Black
Liberation and Gay and Women's Liberation Movements." The underdeveloped plot and characters
are "attributed to the period in which it was
written, where there were no large mass movements
of Lesbians or militant Blacks or...Black Lesbian
Liberation."

B41. Steinman, Esther. Women's Studies: A Recommended
Core Bibliography. Littleton: Libraries Unlimited,
1979. 347.

Regards Loving Her as a contrived novel that "gives
fictional representation to the experience of lesbian mothers and lesbian artists."

B42. Schultz, Elizabeth. "Out of the Woods and into
the World: A Study of Interracial Friendships
between Women in American Novels." Conjuring: Black
Women, Fiction, and Literary Tradition, ed. Marjorie
Pryse and Hortense J. Spillers. Bloomington: Indiana
UP, 1985. 80-81.

Places Shockley's Loving Her with other novels
written by white women who focus on interracial
friendships. Similar to Allison Mill's Francisco
(1974), Loving Her does not explore "the racial
dimension of the interracial friendship"; instead,
it "reflects the destructive potential of sexism"
to the interracial friendship. Such treatment in
literature, says Schultz, reveals that experiences
of white women are relevant to those of black women.

REVIEWS OF SAY JESUS AND COME TO ME

B43. Taylor, Rebecca Sue. Library Journal 107 (1 May
      1982): 906.

      Acknowledges the theme as "the triple handicap
      of being female, lesbian, and black," and lauds
      the novel for its "unique perspective of gay life."
      The primary fault found is several unresolved plot
      lines, but these are not elaborated on.

B44. Strachan, Don. Los Angeles Times Book Review 4
      July 1982: 8.

      Commends Shockley for sensitively exposing sexism,
      black oppression, and homosexuality, but comments
      that she does not focus enough on tensions in the
      characters' relationships.

B45. Monteagudo, Jesse. Weekly News 7 July 1982: 28.

      Compares briefly Shockley's Say Jesus and Come
      to Me with Carol Ann Douglas' To the Cleveland
      Station and concludes that Shockley is a better
      novelist. To Shockley's credit are her superb
      contrasts between Travis Lee and Myrtle Black,
      her "good portrait" of the black church's role
      in the lives of black Americans, and her illumina-
      tion of black lesbian lifestyles. Monteagudo be-
      lieves if there is a flaw in the novel, it is
      Shockley's unsympathetic portrayal of men as
      "arrogant pimps, hypocritical preachers and timid
      faggots."

B46. Gabree, John. Newsday 29 Aug. 1982, sec. Ideas:
      15.

      Praises the novel for its "Unexpected pleasure"
      and good character portrayals, but warns that it
      "may offend some churchgoers." Gabree recommends
      the novel to anyone wanting "an entertaining read"
      and to anyone reading fiction "to visit exotic
      social locales."

B47. Morrison, Joanna. Woman's City County Chronicle
      8 (Aug.-Sept. 1982): 3.

      Notes that in writing an exciting and inspiring
      novel, Shockley has given us powerful characters
      and has exhibited her courage.

B48. Crew, Louie. Advocate [San Mateo] 16 Sept. 1982:
      56.

      Describes Say Jesus and Come to Me as an engaging
      novel that "would make a truly first-rate movie."
      Its interest lies not only in its "potboiler" ef-
      fect, but also in Shockley's expose of fraud.

Her vision of life among blacks and whites,
straights and gays, may cause her to risk friends
and reviewers, especially blacks, but what she
says is refreshing, unbiased, and essentially truth-
ful. In this novel, "Shockley does a superb job
of hiding where it belongs the evidence that she
is indeed an accomplished scholar and a major black
historian."

B49. Tremaine, John S. <u>West Coast Review of Books</u> 8
      (Sept.-Oct. 1982): 66.

      Criticizes the novel for its poor characterization;
      however, much of the criticism stems from Tremaine's
      misreading. He fails to see a clear ethnic identi-
      fication of Reverend Myrtle Black, mistakenly labels
      all the novel's characters as "gay in one form
      or another," and misreads all the male characters
      as "fools or morons." It comes as no surprise
      that a careless reading would enable Tremaine to
      conclude that "Shockley handles her material with
      the ineptitude of Reverend Black's first date.
      Pathetic."

B50. Cahill, Rosemary. <u>Empty Closet</u> 131 (Oct. 1982):
      12.

      Considers Shockley's novel a sensitive and moving
      account of the lesbian condition. Shockley portrays
      Reverend Black as the Elmer Gantry type using "holy
      rhetoric," but she is not stereotyped. Cahill con-
      siders the best scenes to be those of eroticism
      and praises Shockley for coming down hard on racism
      and sexism. Regarding Shockley as an "impressive
      writer," Cahill says Shockley has made some "power-
      ful statements" in this novel.

B51. Newman, Richard. <u>Newsletter</u> of the Afro-American
      Religious History Group of the American Academy
      of Religion, 7 (Fall 1982): 13.

      Views <u>Say Jesus and Come to Me</u> as having good
      material "to make a marvelous movie." The "striking
      and insightful" subjects mentioned in passing are
      the black bourgeoisie, black underworld, black
      music, black church, women's movement, and black
      gay life. The remarks coming from this religious
      history group avoid caustic criticism regarding
      Shockley's unconventional treatment of the black
      church.

B52. Eisenbach, Helen. <u>New York Native</u> 2 (22-Nov.- 5
      Dec. 1982): 39.

      Hesitates to brand the novel a love story or a
      call to sisterhood, but labels it a "peculiar,
      dreadfully written, yet somehow fascinating trashy
      novel...about a lusty, vaguely evil lesbian minis-
      ter...." For those seeking "consistency, meaning,

even eroticism," Eisenbach suggests looking elsewhere. For those seeking a language blended with
the holy and profane, their prayers have been
answered. Such a novel "will not soon come again."

B53.   Joyce, Donald Franklin. _Tennessean_ [Nashville]
       26 Dec. 1982, Sunday Bookcase: F10.

       Considers the women's movement in Nashville as
       the focal point of this novel with Myrtle Black,
       "a charismatic, articulate and beautiful black
       lady minister," advancing the narrative. The women,
       black and white, are viewed as wanting "to liberate
       themselves from myths and traditional restraints"
       imposed upon them by the South and by America
       generally. Racism, male chauvinism, and drug addic-
       tion are oddly rated by Joyce as "subordinate
       themes," oddly because these are the major culprits
       Shockley's women are fighting against.

B54.   Vermij, Lucie Th. _Homologie_ Jan. 1983: 37.

       Compares Myrtle Black to a Billy Graham type, except
       that Myrtle's speeches flow from a deep compassion
       for and understanding of the situation women find
       themselves in. Vermij is not sure whether Myrtle's
       sexuality is of prime importance or whether it
       is strictly due to the rich fantasy of the author.
       In any case, Vermij says Shockley has worked
       Myrtle's sexuality up into a ridiculous story so
       that the reader, from beginning to end, is capti-
       vated and cannot put the book down.

B55.   Unsigned. _Atalanta_ 11 (Feb. 1983): 8.

       Identifies and applauds the character Travis Lee
       as the one to aid Myrtle Black with her pioneering
       women's movement and in crossing over "from being
       an invisible lesbian to...a visible one."

B56.   Clay, Ernest. "Black and White." _New York Native_
       14-27 Feb. 1983: 3.

       Responds to Helen Eisenbach's _New York Native_ review
       of _Say Jesus and Come to Me_. Clay calls it "dis-
       tressing" that Eisenbach misreported Travis Lee's
       identity as "a white country musician" when she
       is "a black blues singer." He reminds Eisenbach
       that she completely ignored the analysis in the
       novel of the way white women "attempt to matronize
       and thus co-opt black leaders" and that she "could
       find herself sipping cocktails by the swimming
       pool described in the novel, as she establishes
       her credentials as a silly gossip who gives a false
       report."

B57.   Eisenbach, Helen. "Black and White." _New York Native_
       14-27 Feb. 1983: 3,4.

Responds to Ernest Clay's asssessment of her review of <u>Say Jesus and Come to Me</u> and places the blame for her misreading the characters on the novel's "incoherence." As for Mr. Clay's notion about "usurping...white women," Eisenbach says his notion seems "self-indulgent and dangerous in a society where power is wielded economically rather than in the curl of a patronizing smile...." She maintains that she read the entire novel and that there are "better books out there begging to be read."

B58.   Clarke, Cheryl, et al. "Black Women on Black Women Writers: Conversations and Questions." <u>Conditions: Nine</u> 3 (Spring 1983): 88-135. [99, 113-14]

Examines in a pentalog <u>Say Jesus and Come to Me</u> and other black feminist books. The basic flaw in Shockley's novel, says Jewelle Gomez, is the portrayal of Reverend Black as "unconscious politically while using political stances purely for her self-aggrandizement." It is the introduction of politics and the failure to develop Reverend Black as a true political figure that cause Linda Powell to question whether the novel is "just bad writing or just bad politics." In any case, Powell views the characters in <u>Say Jesus and Come to Me</u> and in <u>The Black and White of It</u> as "dull" and wonders why Shockley's works are so appealing to white women.

B59.   James, Dot. <u>Our Paper</u> 12 Oct. 1983: 15-16.

Puts <u>Say Jesus and Come to Me</u> "in the tradition of the pulps written in the 1950's, early 1960's by Ann Bannon (Ann Holinquist)." In fact, James regards the name "Ann Shockley" as "Holinquist's pseudonym for the '80's" because of the terminology used in the novel. Not knowing who Ann Shockley is and seeming not to care, James ventures to say that Shockley "smeared burnt cork on her face to write this book," not one word in it about the black experience does James believe. James does not recommend this novel as escape fiction or as eroticism.

B60.   Kulp, Denise E. "We Sisters Have a Legacy of Power." <u>Off Our Backs</u> 14 (Aug.-Sept. 1984): 13.

Says that this novel "is a very fun read." This review lacks critical insight.

B61.   Dandridge, Rita B. "Shockley, the Iconoclast." <u>Callaloo</u> 22 (Fall 1984): 160-64.

Posits the significance of the novel as its iconoclastic attack on the black church which functions as a "mask" for a certain type of unscrupulous black minister. In this vein, the church "becomes

an accomplice in a (social) crime where the exercise
of patriarchalism means pushing the system as far
as it will go in the direction of shunning homosexuals, while capitalizing on and keeping women
in their places." The strength of Reverend Myrtle
Black, the central character, is made evident by
her wearing eccentric, colorful clothing which
openly reveals her protest against traditional
religion and against homophobia. Moreover, un-
married, barren, lesbian, and preacher, she de-
mythicizes the black woman as a "willing conformist
to sexist prejudices operating against her." Important to an understanding of this novel are Shockley's comments: "There will always be more who
dislike the theme than like it. This doesn't bother
me....Black women who want to mollify touchy black
male prides will never attempt to comprehend what
I am saying, nor will insecure black males."

REVIEWS OF LIVING BLACK AMERICAN AUTHORS

B62. Beatty, Floy W. "Fisk Librarians Edit Important
      Volume." Tennessean [Nashville] 6 Jan. 1974: 7B.

      Notes that Living Black American Authors includes
      known and lesser known names of blacks from various
      fields. Entries are arranged alphabetically and
      include: "real name, if pen name is used; occupa-
      tion; place and date of birth; education; marital
      status and children; work experience; memberships
      in organizations and associations; awards received;
      a selected bibliography of published works; and
      current mailing address." Beatty regards as special
      features of this book its title index and directory
      of black publishers.

B63. Unsigned. "Bowker Publishes 1st Directory of Living
      Black American Writers." Louisville Defender 17
      Jan. 1974: A5.

      Emphasizes that Living Black American Authors was
      published exactly two hundred years after the
      appearance of Phillis Wheatley's Poems on Various
      Subjects, Religious and Moral, the first published
      book by a Senegalese-born, resident black American.
      The directory is praised as the first of its kind;
      its variety and comprehensiveness are noted, and
      its list of addresses for black publishers is re-
      garded as a convenience source.

B64. Schuyler, George S. "The Literary Line." Union
      Leader [Manchester, NH] 11 Feb. 1974: 13.

      Notes the requirements for inclusion in this direc-
      tory -- that "the author must be living, black
      American and have had something published, no matter
      where." Schuyler comments that some names listed
      he has never seen before and laughably regards
      as "editorial carelessness or ignorance" the
      omission of George S. Schuyler (his own name),
      who "thankfully is black, an American, and living,
      with four or five books to his name!"

B65. Unsigned. Review of the News 10 (27 Feb. 1974):
      28.

      Refers to Schuyler's review of Living Black American
      Authors and exaggerates the editors' omission of
      Schuyler's name by enumerating his accomplishments.
      This reviewer concludes that "either Shockley and
      Chandler are ignorant of their field or they have
      purposely excluded Mr. Schuyler because he is (as
      the title of his autobiography has it) Black and
      Conservative."

B66.   Unsigned. <u>Booklist</u> 70 (15 Mar. 1974): 753.

Cites <u>Living Black American Authors</u> as "a welcome
addition to biographical collections in libraries"
because information on living black American authors
is difficult to come by. Mention is made of 450
authors included and of twenty black publishers
appended. Although favorable, the review does note
that "information for some authors (was taken)
from printed sources" and "in print status is not
indicated" for works listed.

B67.   Kaiser, Ernest. <u>Freedomways</u> 14 (First Quarter 1974):
91.

Analyzes <u>Living Black American Authors</u> as a recent
book whose "facts are useful." Kaiser comments
that the format and questions presented in this
directory are more for the professional than for
the self-educated.

B68.   Schenck, William. <u>Library Journal</u> 99 (1 Apr. 1974):
1018, 1020.

Charges that <u>Living Black American Authors</u> is
"unfortunately, quite an unsatisfactory reference
work." His reasons include: authors such as Angela
Davis are omitted, some biographical listings are
incomplete, the black publishers' list is incomplete, and the topography is poor.

B69.   Unsigned. <u>Black Times</u> 4 (6 Apr. 1974): 14.

Reprints most of the review found in <u>Louisville
Defender</u> 17 Jan. 1974: A5.

B70.   Melton, Marie. <u>Catholic Library World</u> 45 (Apr.
1974): 454.

Finds this directory a "worthy addition to a reference collection" and mentions that editors have
already referred to the book's shortcomings in
the Preface. Melton looks forward to subsequent
editions.

B71.   Unsigned. <u>Wilson Library Bulletin</u> 48 (Apr. 1974):
677-78.

Praises the directory for its scope, its definition
of "author," its useful mailing list, and its title
index.

B72.   Unsigned. <u>Reference Service Review</u> 2 (Apr.-June
1974): 18.

Cites the directory as an excellent source for
hard-to-find information.

B73. Unsigned. <u>Choice</u> 11 (May 1974): 416.

Recognizes this work as a "pioneer effort" intended "to serve librarians and others seeking concise data about the authors' background and work." Mention is made that the compilers "confess the possibility of error" and did make errors, one of which is the inclusion of Bernard Mandel, a non-black.

B74. Kilgore, James C. <u>Black World</u> 33 (June 1974): 86-88.

Points out that the limited number of authors included is owing to the fact that "an author listed... is one who saw and responded to the appeal for data in one of the periodicals where the announcement of the forthcoming directory appeared." Kilgore says the compilers should have "consulted with editors of Black journals and publishing firms...anthologies of contemporary literature... and recent comprehensive bibliographies." He refers to incomplete and inconsistent entries and says that the directory "would have been vastly improved if more time had been used in its preparation and development."

B75. Wynkoop, Sally. <u>American Reference Books Annual</u> 6 (1975): 599.

Contends that "a good biographical directory of black authors is needed. But this isn't it." Wynkoop finds coverage uneven and well-known writers omitted.

REVIEWS OF <u>HANDBOOK OF BLACK LIBRARIANSHIP</u>

B76.   Unsigned. <u>Interracial Books for Children</u> 9.8 (1978):
       20.

       Cites the <u>Handbook</u> as containing "essays on pioneers
       and landmark episodes in Black librarianship [as
       well as] vital issues, significant books and peri-
       odicals for Black collections...."

B77.   Unsigned. <u>American Reference Book Annual</u> 9 (1978):
       81.

       Gives a good description of the <u>Handbook</u> and
       asserts that "contemporary black librarianship
       is well covered."

B78.   Gore, George W. "First Definitive Handbook of Black
       Librarianship." <u>Nashville Banner</u> 28 Jan. 1978,
       sec. 1: 5.

       Maintains that <u>Handbook of Black Librarianship</u>
       is the first definitive handbook of black librarian-
       ship with certain positive aspects: (1) it recog-
       nizes black Americans' past and present contribu-
       tions to libraries, (2) it identifies materials
       essential to Afro-American collections, and (3)
       it names branches of public library systems serving
       predominantly black communities.

B79.   Collins, L. M. <u>Tennessean</u> [Nashville] 19 Mar. 1978,
       Sunday Bookcase: F10.

       Couples and reviews Shockley's <u>Handbook of Black
       Librarianship</u> and Jessie Carney Smith's <u>Black
       Academic Libraries and Research Collections</u>. Collins
       recognizes both books as "voices of authority raised
       to insist on maintaining adequate library services
       and strengthening educational facilities through
       a 'thorough and up-to-date analysis of library
       programs' in colleges whose philosophies are girded
       by democratic principles of education for Everyman."

B80.   Smith, Jessie Cottman. <u>College and Research
       Libraries</u> 39 (May 1978): 223-24.

       Praises this book for its thoroughness, organi-
       zation, and clear and readable style. Updating
       is encouraged where statistics are given.

B81.   Unsigned. <u>Booklist</u> 74 (15 May 1978): 1519.

       Gives a thorough descriptive overview of the
       <u>Handbook</u> and presents it as "comprehensive and
       well-written... [and] a much-needed, interesting
       mine of information on past and present black
       librarianship." The <u>Handbook</u> is current "as of
       mid-1977."

B82.   Totten, Herman L. "Weapons against Intolerance and Ignorance: A Review Essay." <u>Journal of Library History, Philosophy and Comparative Librarianship</u> 13 (Summer 1978): 304-09.

Quotes President Lyndon B. Johnson in 1963 as saying, "Books and ideas are the most effective weapons against intolerance and ignorance" as a springboard for examining Shockley and Josey's <u>Handbook of Black Librarianship</u> and Jessie Smith's <u>Black Academic Libraries and Research Collections</u>. Both books are regarded as the most effective weapons against ignorance "to come to the forefront in recent times," and the <u>Handbook</u> is referred to as a "survival manual." Totten appreciates the "magnitude of the effort" necessary to complete the <u>Handbook</u> and commends the editors for their devotion to a task completed without release time from their jobs and without monetary assistance. Since the information compiled in the <u>Handbook</u> would take considerable time for an individual to obtain from various sources, Totten suggests that the <u>Handbook</u> be considered and read as a "compendium of knowledge, a one-volume encyclopedia."

B83.   Biddle, Stanton. <u>Journal of Academic Librarianship</u> 4 (Sept. 1978): 229, 251.

Presents the <u>Handbook</u> as "a wealth of hitherto obscure or uncompiled data on people, events, and resources." Among the essays read, Biddle finds Charles L. Blackson's "Experiences of a Black Private Book Collector" to be "especially inspirational."

B84.   Jones, Virginia Lacy. <u>Library Quarterly</u> 49 (Jan. 1979): 103-04.

Affirms that "black librarians...were pioneers in developing library services for all races at the national, state, and local levels, while at the same time they struggled in a hostile society to overcome barriers of racial segregation to make libraries accessible to all." What Lacy sees as especially important about this work is that it chronicles the contributions black librarians have made to librarianship generally in the face of obstacles. It provides, moreover, "ready access to information" not previously collected and difficult to locate.

B85.   Unsigned. <u>Journal of Academic Librarianship</u> 4 (Jan. 1979): 459.

Identifies the <u>Handbook of Black Librarianship</u> as "a landmark volume on a subject that heretofore has been almost invisible and certainly inaccessible to many librarians." Among the extremely important

sections of the book are mentioned black collections, special children's services, and library
services to black Americans. The book is highly
recommended for reading.

B86.   Unsigned. Best reference Book: 1970-1980. Littleton:
Libraries Unlimited, 1981. 111.

Cites review in American Reference Book Annual
7 (1978): 81.

IV.
ANN ALLEN SHOCKLEY:
BIOGRAPHY
AND CRITICISM

BIOGRAPHY AND CRITICISM IN NEWSPAPERS

B87. "Negro Leader Here Dies, Rites Set for Tomorrow."
Courier Journal [Louisville] 17 Mar. 1944, sec. 2:
2.

Gives the obituary notice for Bessie L. Allen, Shockley's mother. Mrs. Allen, who was the first black social
worker in Louisville, Kentucky, died at fifty-eight
years old on March 15, 1944. She was also the first
black probation officer in the Louisville Juvenile
Court, established the Kentucky Home Society for Colored
Children, and was a delegate to President Hoover's
White House Conference on Child Health and Welfare.

B88. "Miss Ann E. Allen Weds in Maryland." Louisville
Defender 17 Sept. 1949: 10.

Announces Shockley's marriage to William Shockley,
in Elkton, Maryland, August 29, 1949. The couple honey-
mooned in Philadelphia and started their home in Milford, Delaware.

B89. "Mrs. Ann Shockley Gets Scholarship for Library Degree."
Bridgeville News [DE] 19 Sept. 1958: 1.

Announces Shockley's having been awarded a scholarship
by the Graduate School of Library Science at Western
Reserve University, in Cleveland, Ohio, to pursue a
year's study for a master's degree in Library Science.

B90. "Mrs. Shockley Seeks School Board Seat." Bridgeville
News [DE] 12 May 1960: 1.

Mentions Shockley will file for election, May 14, 1960,
as a member of the Board of Trustees of the Phillis
Wheatley School. Before Shockley, there have been no
women on the Phillis Wheatley School Board to seek

a seat. Shockley's intention is indicative of her belief
that "there is a need for re-examination of the school's
program along with stimulating greater community interest and a stronger liaison between board members,
faculty members, and community to enhance and broaden
the school's educational sights."

B91.   "Mrs. Shockley Receives Grant for Research Paper."
       Bridgeville News [DE] 10 June 1960: 1.

Notice of Shockley's receiving a grant from the Research
Committee at Delaware State College to write a research
paper entitled "A History of Public Library Services
to Negroes in the South." Owing to the scareness and
value of the materials included in the study, a copy
of the completed project will be distributed to library
associations throughout the country.

B92.   "Ann Shockley Completes Survey." Bridgeville News
       [DE] 9 June 1961: 1.

Announces Shockley's completion and publication of
a survey of Special Negro Collections in predominantly
Negro libraries. The title of the study is "Does the
Negro College Library Need a Special Negro Collection?"
The study has been published in the June 1961 issue
of Library Journal.

B93.   "Mrs. Ann Shockley Wins 1st in Short Story Contest."
       Bridgeville News [DE] 11 May 1962: 1.

Notice of Shockley's winning first prize for her short
story "The Picture Prize" in the Annual Writing Project
sponsored by the American Association of University
Women. She was among 133 participants. A photograph
of Shockley is included.

B94.   Garber, Eric. "Taint Nobody's Business: Homosexuality
       in Harlem in the 1920's." Advocate [San Mateo] 13 May
       1982: 53.

Thanks Shockley as a librarian for assisting him in
the preparation of his article.

B95.   "Tamara Shockley Is an Attorney at United Nations."
       Seaford Leader [DE] 3 Nov. 1984: A16.

Announces that Tamara Shockley, the daughter of Ann
Allen Shockley and the late William L. Shockley, was
the "sole black student to attend Bridgeville's school
... [and] today, she is an attorney-at-law." Tamara
Shockley's educational background and professional
employment are given.

BIOGRAPHY AND CRITICISM IN PERIODICALS

B96.   Fisk News: Alumni Magazine 40 (Summer 1966): 25.

Mentions Shockley as an assistant librarian at Maryland
State College, Princess Anne, Maryland.

B97.   Maryland State College News 1 (Apr. 1967): 1.

A rare photograph appears of Shockley, who stands
third from the left with the library staff of Maryland
State College during the ground breaking ceremony
for the new Frederick Douglass Library.

B98.   Maryland State College News 17 (May 1969): 4-6.

Makes known Shockley's resignation as librarian at
Maryland State College, her contributions such as
giving direction to Readers' Services and publishing
Library News, her forthcoming works to be published,
her attendance at Negro Culture Institute in Salisbury,
and her lecture on "The Use of the Library" to Upward
Bound Students at Maryland State College.

B99.   Black World 20 (Jan. 1971): 65.

Following the short story "Is She Relevant?" Shockley
is cited as an associate librarian and head of Special
Collections at Fisk University.

B100. Unsigned. American Libraries 3 (Sept. 1972): 850.

An announcement about Fisk University sponsoring a
three-day Black Oral History Conference in Nashville,
Tennessee. Shockley is coordinator of the program.

B101. North, Dennis. American Reference Books Annual, 1973
392.

Announces the publication of Fisk Jubilee Singers:
Centennial Year, 1871-1971 as volume two of a series
called BANC! an acronym for Black, Afro-American,
Negro, Colored. BANC! is edited by Shockley and is
"an accessions list of books added to the Special
Collection of the Fisk University Library."

B102. Soul 7 (26 Feb. 1973): 6.

Comments on the eighteen-minute black and white film
entitled Blood's Way, based on Shockley's short story
"Crying for Her Man." The film is regarded as the
finest to emerge from American Film Institute during
1972; it features Tracy Reed as star. The film was
shown at a Los Angeles theater prior to the Academy
Awards and will be entered as an Oscar contender.

B103.   Unsigned. "From Woodville to Greystone: The Odyssey
        of a Young Black Film Maker." AFI Report 3 (Nov. 1973):
        9-11.

        Announcement of Stan Taylor's film production of Ann
        Allen Shockley's "Crying for Her Man." The film is
        called Blood's Way.

B104.   7 Fisk Women Writers Feb. 1974: 4.

        Shockley is recognized with other Fisk University
        women writers such as Nikki Giovanni, Nella Larsen,
        and Sarah Webster Fabio. Her works cited are Living
        Black American Authors (1973), A History of Public
        Library Services to Negroes in the South, 1900-1955,
        and The Administration of Special Black Collections
        (1970).

B105.   Fisk Friday 22 Feb. 1974: 3.

        Announces the publication of Ann Allen Shockley's
        Living Black American Authors: A Biographical Directory
        and the forthcoming publication of two essays, "Black
        Book Reviewing: A Case for Library Action" and "The
        New Black Feminists."

B106.   Smith, Barbara. "Toward a Black Feminist Criticism."
        Conditions: Two 1 (Oct. 1977): 25-44.

        Documents the general failure of the literary world
        to recognize black women and black lesbian writers
        and calls for a black feminist criticism to articulate
        the politics of race, sex, and class in black women's
        works. Such a stance will offset the negative criticism
        and reveal that black women writers "constitute an
        identifiable literary tradition." Using Toni Morrison's
        Sula, Smith shows how a black feminist critical per-
        spective gives a lesbian interpretation to Sula and
        Nel's behavior, and how such an interpretation adds
        another level of meaning to the novel. Finally, Smith
        praises black women writers such as Audre Lorde, Pat
        Parker, and Ann Allen Shockley, who have dared to
        write about lesbians and, in doing so, have necessi-
        tated a "reassessment of black literature and literary
        history...to reveal the black woman-identified woman."

B107.   Bibliophage 92 (Spring 1978): 9.

        Cites Shockley as an alumna of the School of Library
        Science at Case Western Reserve University and as
        co-author of Handbook of Black Librarianship.

B108.   Jet 54 (24 Aug. 1978): 60.

        Announces the intended production of Shockley's short
        story "The World of Rosie Polk" as a two-hour televi-
        sion movie by Rollaway Productions, formed by Esther
        Rolle. Joe Hubbard, Jr. and Stan Taylor will produce

the film, and Taylor and Shockley are writing the screen play. The screen version will portray a southern black woman and her son struggling against odds for survival. (Internal difficulties at Rollaway Productions prevented the production of Shockley's story.)

B109.   Kaiser, Ernest. Freedomways 18 (Third Quarter 1978): 175.

Lists Handbook of Black Librarianship among recent books published and states that it "has pulled together all of the scattered material in magazines and other places relating to black libraries and black librarians." Kaiser notes that "it will still be a useful reference book years from now when its lists will need updating."

B110.   Dandridge, Rita B. "Male Critics/Black Women's Novels." CLA Journal 23 (Sept. 1979): 1-11.

Defends Shockley's Loving Her against Frank Lamont Phillips' attack of it as "trash." Dandridge categorizes Phillips as a paternalistic male critic who resists change by trying to regulate subject matter in black women's novels. Owing to "the new sexual liberation and the breakdown in some racial taboos facing America in the 1970's" when Loving Her was published, Phillips' stance is unrealistic, says Dandridge. She calls for a breed of critic apart from Phillips to assess the subjects black women novelists write about. This new critic must consider, at least, the woman writer's purpose, methodology, temperament, and social circumstances.

B111.   Cornwell, Anita. "To the Sisters of the Azalea Collective and Lesbians Rising -- A Thank You Note for the Second Annual Third World Lesbian Writers' Conference on April 12, 1980, at Hunter College, New York, New York." Sinister Wisdom 13 (Spring 1980): 43-44.

Cornell extends her thanks for many inspirations she received while attending this conference. She says that one of the high moments of the panel she participated on was a "stirring message" from Ann Allen Shockley, read by Audre Lorde, which urged us "to create and promote our own publishing modus operandi, markets and readership.... The time is ripe, the hour is here...."

B112.   "Whom Do You Write For? A Collage." Sinister Wisdom 13 (Spring 1980): 36.

Responding to the question, "Whom do you write for?" Shockley answers: "I write for anybody who elects to read my work. I do this with the hope that the message I am trying to impart, for there is always one, will come through clearly, and cause readers to think more perceptively, try to initiate changes, and learn to accept different races, as well as individuals within them."

B113.   White, Evelyn C. "Comprehensive Oppression: Lesbians and Race in the Work of Ann Allen Shockley." Backbone 3 (1981): 38-40.

Shares favorable and unfavorable opinions about Loving Her and The Black and White of It, both of which are "firsts" in their genre to focus on the subject of lesbianism as viewed by a black woman. White implies that there is development of theme, characters, and language in the latter of the two works, but that both convey the "comprehensive oppression" of lesbians. This oppression is evident in the fact that the lesbian "suffers from a lack of an objective literary identity and exposure; that the notions that do exist about her are distorted and misconceived; and that homophobia [exists] in the community."

B114.   Segrest, M. "Lines I Dare to Write: Lesbian Writing in the South." Southern Exposure 9 (Summer 1981): 53-62.

Includes Shockley among southern lesbian fiction writers whose works "claim [women's] sadness and... separations." Segrest sees the loneliness that is so much an aspect of this sadness in Loving Her and The Black and White of It, where Shockley writes of various separations: "black from white, straight from homosexual, old from young, and dyke from new lesbian." Shockley's writings exude her pain rather than her anger at these separations and her "wish for a different wholeness."

B115.   Jet 63 (13 Sept. 1982): 30.

Congratulates Shockley for the publication of her novel Say Jesus and Come to Me.

B116.   Kaiser, Ernest. Freedomways 23 (Fourth Quarter 1983): 301.

Notice of Say Jesus and Come to Me as a recent book published by the same author of Loving Her, Living Black American Authors, and Handbook of Black Librarianship. Kaiser mentions that Shockley is associate librarian for public services and associate professor of library science at Fisk University.

B117.   Streeter, Caroline. "Black Feminist Anthology." Off Our Backs 14 (Aug.-Sept. 1984): 10-11.

Questions Jewelle L. Gomez's castigation of Ann Allen Shockley in the essay "A Cultural Legacy Denied and Discovered: Black Lesbians in Fiction by Women," which appeared in Barbara Smith's anthology Home Girls. Even though Streeter admits she has not read Shockley's Say Jesus and Come to Me, she takes issue with Gomez who alleges that Shockley's portrayal of black lesbians in the novel is "trivial." The reason for Streeter's response is the close proximity in Smith's anthology

of Gomez's article to that of Shockley's, "The Black
Lesbian in American Literature: An Overview," in which
Shockley "clearly demonstrates her committment to
and impressive knowledge of Black feminist literature
and poetry."

B118.   Hernton, Calvin. "The Sexual Mountain and Black Women
Writers." Black American Literature Forum 18 (Winter
1984): 139-145.

Writes poignantly of the sexual mountain black women
writers have had to "pound" to make noticeable their
works in a literary world dominated by chauvinism.
With quiet respect, Hernton includes Ann Shockley
with other pioneering feminist writers such as Toni
Cade Bambara, Barbara Smith, and Alice Walker. He
respects them as "critics, scholars, intellectuals,
and ideologues of our times" who because of their
writings (Shockley's Loving Her, for instance) have
had to withstand such abusive labels as "feminist
bitches" and "black-men-haters" from black male critics. Such labels come from "threatened" black men
responding to black women writers "declaring their
independence,...gaining autonomous influence,...
causing their existence to be seen and felt...in areas
heretofore barred to them... and wrestling recognition
from the white literary powers that be." The writings
of these women are "the negation of the negative,"
a proffering of a vision "of unfettered human possibility."

B119.   Bogus, SDiane. "On Ann Allen Shockley and Black Lesbians in American Literature." Mama Bears News and
Notes 2 (Oct.-Nov. 1985): 7+.

Traces the movement of Shockley's major fictions from
the "semi-romantic portrayal of a life of bliss for
the middle-class Black lesbian...to inside views of
the black lesbian in relationship to the family, in
relationship to the woman's community, and in relationship to their careers." Such progressive development
of her works entitles Shockley to better critical
reviews of her fiction than she has received, says
Bogus, who intends to rectify this negative critical
reception in her doctoral dissertation on Ann
Shockley's fictions.

BIOGRAPHY AND CRITICISM IN BOOKS

B120.   A Biographical Directory of Librarians in U.S. and
        Canada. Ed. Lee Ash. 5th ed. Chicago: American Library
        Association, 1970. 1000.

        Contains a brief biographical sketch of Ann Allen
        Shockley.

B121.   Dictionary of International Biography. 7th ed. London:
        Melrose, 1970. Pt. 2: 1008.

        Gives Shockley's professional appointments and member-
        ships.

B122.   Directory of Afro-American Resources. Ed. Walter
        Schatz. New York: Bowker, 1970. 303.

        Cites Shockley as the person who collected poet Naomi
        Long Madgett's papers for Special Collections at Fisk
        University.

B123.   Randall, Ann Knight. "Dreams, Reality, and Tailor-
        Made Service." What Black Librarians Are Saying.
        Ed. E. J. Josey. Metuchen: Scarecrow, 1972: 294.

        Announces that Shockley's A Handbook for the Adminis-
        tration of Special Black Collections is an important
        available manual for those librarians working with
        black collections. The manual was developed at Fisk
        University "for the special institutes in Black Studies
        Librarianship."

B124.   Shockley, Ann Allen, and Sue P. Chandler, eds. Living
        Black American Authors: A Biographical Directory.
        New York: Bowker, 1973. 144-45.

        Omits date of birth from Shockley's biographical sketch
        which includes professional experiences, awards, and
        some publications through 1971.

B125.   The World Who's Who of Women. 1st ed. Cambridge, Eng.:
        Melrose, 1973. 1: 791.

        Includes Shockley's professional appointments, publi-
        cations, contributions to newspapers, memberships,
        and honors.

B126.   Rhodes, Lelia G. "A Critical Analysis of the Career
        Backgrounds of Selected Black Female Librarians."
        DAI 36 (1975): 3190 A. Florida State U.

        Ann Allen Shockley is included among fifteen black
        librarians whose career backgrounds were analyzed
        for this investigation. The study reveals, among other
        pertinent information, that the respondents came from

middle class Southern backgrounds, they attended the top library schools in the country, they majored either in English or history in undergraduate school, and "librarianship was not the primary career choice."

B127.   Community Leaders and Noteworthy Americans. Ed. J. T. Vickers. Raleigh: American Biographical Institute, 1975. 792.

Lists Shockley's professional experiences and memberships in professional organizations.

B128.   Contemporary Authors: A Bio-Bibliographical Guide to Current Authors and Their Works. Ed. Clare D. Kinsman. Detroit: Gale, 1975. 49-52: 493-94.

Contains general bio-biliographical material on Ann Allen Shockley.

B129.   Rush, Theressa Gunnels, et al, eds. Black American Writers Past and Present: A Biographical and Bibliographical Dictionary. Metuchen: Scarecrow, 1975. 2: 664.

Gives a brief biographical sketch and lists Shockley's works under categories of autobiography, criticism, editor, novel, and short stories.

B130.   Who's Who of American Women, 1975-1976. 9th ed. Chicago: Marquis Who's Who, 1975. 812.

Lists Shockley's professional experiences, awards, and some publications.

B131.   Directory of Ethnic Studies Librarians. Comp. Beth J. Shapiro. Chicago: Office for Library Services to the Disadvantaged American Library Association, 1976. 66.

Includes Shockley's employment, rank, and interests. Among her interests are the collection and preservation of secondary and primary sources relative to black history and culture, personal research and writing on blacks, presenting lectures, editing, serving as consultant, and black books reviewing.

B132.   Margolies, Edward, and David Bakish, eds. Afro-American Fiction, 1853-1976. Detroit: Gale, 1976. 92.

Of Living Black American Authors, Margolies and Bakish say that it "does not include a number of authors."

B133.   Who's Who among Black Americans. Ed William C. Matney. 1st ed. Northbrook, IL: Inc. 1976. 1: 566. 2nd ed. 1978. 1: 81. 3rd ed. 721.

Lists Ann Shockley as a black books evaluator and consultant for black collections. Each successive edition updates Shockley's achievements.

B134. The Writers' Directory, 1976-1978. New York: St.
       Martin's, 1976. 978.

       Includes Shockley's educational and professional
       experiences and lists her as editor of American
       Library Association's Black Caucus Newsletter since
       1972.

B135. Josey, J. E., and Ann Allen Shockley, comps. Handbook
       of Black Librarianship. Littleton: Libraries Unlimited,
       1977. 22,23, 41, 163-64, 248, 253.

       Mentions that the first oral history conference held
       at Fisk University in 1972 was under Ann Shockley's
       direction. Acknowledges Shockley's on-going efforts
       to build the black oral history collection at Fisk
       University. Includes among Shockley's achievements
       the special award bestowed upon her in 1975 by the
       American Library Association's Black Caucus for her
       services as first editor of the Black Caucus News-
       letter.

B136. Page, James A., comp. Selected Black American Authors:
       An Illustrated Bio-Bibliography. Boston: G.K. Hall,
       1977. 2: 249.

       Includes bio-bibliographical information found in
       Shockley and Chandler's Living Black American Authors.

B137. Fairbanks, Carol, and Eugene A. Engeldinger, eds.
       Black American Fiction: A Bibliography. Metuchen:
       Scarecrow, 1978. 253-54.

       Includes biography, criticism, minor fiction, and
       comments on Loving Her.

B138. Spradling, Mary Mace, ed. In Black and White. 3rd
       ed. Detroit: Gale, 1980. 2: 873.

       Cites Ann Shockley as a biographer (apparently in
       connection with her oral history project at Fisk Uni-
       versity) and lists other references with biographical
       holdings on Shockley.

B139. Encyclopedia of Black America. Eds. Augustus W. Low
       and Virgil A. Clift. New York: McGraw-Hill, 1981.
       753.

       Contains a one-paragraph biographical sketch which
       incorrectly lists Ann Shockley's birth year as 1925.

B140. Roberts, J. R. Black Lesbians: An Annotated Biblio-
       graphy. Tallahassee: Naiad, 1981. 18, 24, 35, 41-44,
       64, 68-69, 73.

       Includes nineteen bibliographical annotations of works
       about and by Ann Allen Shockley.

B141. Cruikshank, Margaret, ed. Lesbian Studies: Present and Future. Old Westbury: Feminist P, 1982. 59, 103, 107, 147, 151.

Scattered references appear regarding Shockley's Loving Her and The Black and White of It. Mentions that Shockley's lesbian fiction published after 1974 was written before 1970, that her short story collection The Black and White of It is recommended reading in women's studies courses. Cruikshank says that it is debatable whether the short story collection is feminist fiction or not.

B142. Who's Who in Library and Information Service. Ed. Joel M. Lee. Chicago: American Library Association, 1982. 2: 454.

Lists Ann Allen Shockley's educational and professional experiences and major publications until 1977.

B143. A Directory of American Poets and Fiction Writers. New York: Poets and Writers, 1983. 175.

Includes Shockley's most recent fiction.

B144. Gomez, Jewelle. "A Cultural Legacy Denied and Discovered: Black Lesbians in Fiction by Women." Home Girls: A Black feminsit Anthology. Ed. Barbara Smith. New York: Kitchen Table: Women of Color P, 1983. 110-23.

Mentions the general invisibility of black lesbian characters in fiction and reveals that black women who write about lesbians are "routinely ignored by publishing." Gomez considers Shockley's Loving Her "a groundbreaking effort whose mere accomplishment deserves applause." Its appearance "opened up the popular market for books with Black lesbians as principal characters." Gomez is not as favorable towards Say Jesus and Come to Me which, she says, borders on the "Twilight Girl school of literature"; that is, it is "titillation literature." Generally, Gomez views Shockley's works as "trivializing Black Lesbians and their sexuality and [painting] a picture of an unremittingly irrelevant feminist movement." Shockley's mistake is the same one made by her white counterparts, says Gomez: "the inability to place a Black lesbian in a believable cultural context in an artful way."

B145. The Writers Directory: 1984-1986. Chicago: St. James, 1983. 889.

Capsules recent bio-bibliographical information on Ann Allen Shockley.

B146. Houston, Helen R. "Ann Allen Shockley." Dictionary of Literary Biography: Afro-American Fiction Writers after 1955. Eds. Thadious M. Davis and Trudier Harris. Detroit: Gale, 1984. 33: 232-35.

This is the first biographical-literary essay written
about Ann Allen Shockley; it traces her interest in
writing since the eighth grade, reveals her writing
process, and notes her strengths and weaknesses as
a writer. Shockley is considered a "versatile thematic
contemporary writer" whose main concern in exploring
such themes as racism, sexism, and homophobia is "to
encourage readers to accept life experiences as they
really are, without condemnation based on moral codes
that have emanated from the minds of people with narrow
vision." Her first novel Loving Her "opened new vistas
in Afro-American literature," but it has not obtained
the popularity of her nonfiction; this lack of acceptance Shockley attributes to "the subject matter which
is avant-garde and the immediate wants of mainstream
publishers." Houston says Shockley's fiction is ignored
generally by black critics, with the exception of
Alice Walker, Nellie McKay, and Rita Dandridge, "who
have objectively viewed her works."

B147.   Koppelman, Susan, ed. Between Mothers and Daughters.
         New York: Feminist P, 1985. 285-86.

General critical assessment of Ann Allen Shockley's
feminist fiction precedes the short story "A Birthday
Remembered." Koppelman views Shockley's fiction as
dealing "with how the lives of individual and coupled
black heterosexuals -- mostly middle-class -- and
black and racially unidentified lesbians are short-
circuited by racism, sexism, and homophobia." Shockley
explores such themes as shared oppression, social
invisibility, and erosion of hope. Her writing is
personal, but implies the political.

B148.   Harris, Trudier. "Black Writers in a Changed Landscape,
         since 1950." The History of Southern Literature. Ed.
         Louis D. Rubin, et al. Baton Rouge: Louisiana State
         UP, 1985. 571.

Cites Shockley's Loving Her as one of the few novels
written by a Southern black woman treating the lesbian
theme. Harris writes, "Shockley's novel is Southern
more in its writer's origins than in its development
of theme or in its scenery."

INDEX

Included in this general subject index are the titles of primary and secondary works, co-authors and editors of primary works, authors of secondary works, and titles and persons referred to in primary and secondary works. The numbers following each name or title refer the reader to entry numbers in the bibliography. Entry numbers prefixed with "A" denote primary works, and those prefixed with "B," secondary works.

ABOUT THE COMPILER

RITA B. DANDRIDGE is Professor of English at Norfolk State University, Virginia. She co-authored *Relevant Expository Techniques and Programmed Grammar*, has published articles in numerous journals, including the *CLA Journal*, *MELUS*, and *Callaloo*, and has published essays in both *But Some of Us Are Brave* and the *Dictionary of Literary Biography: Afro-American Fiction Writers After 1955*.

www.ingramcontent.com/pod-product-compliance
Lightning Source LLC
Chambersburg PA
CBHW021539260326
41914CB00001B/78